Instant Pot
Indian

70 FULL-FLAVOR, AUTHENTIC RECIPES
FOR ANY SIZED INSTANT POT

ANUPY SINGLA

S
SURREY
BOOKS

AN AGATE IMPRINT

CHICAGO

First printed in April 2023

Printed in China

10 9 8 7 6 5 4 3 2 1   23 24 25 26 27

Library of Congress Cataloging-in-Publication Data
Names: Singla, Anupy, author.
Title: Instant Pot Indian : 70 easy, full-flavor, authentic recipes for any
 sized Instant Pot / Anupy Singla.
Description: Chicago : Surrey, an Agate imprint, [2023] | Includes index. |
 Summary: "Delicious, authentic Indian fare that's quicker and easier
 than ever, with measurements for any sized Instant Pot"-- Provided by
 publisher.
Identifiers: LCCN 2022043497 (print) | LCCN 2022043498 (ebook) | ISBN
 9781572843172 (paperback) | ISBN 9781572848689 (ebook)
Subjects: LCSH: Cooking, Indic. | Smart cookers. | LCGFT: Cookbooks.
Classification: LCC TX724.5.I4 S5349 2023 (print) | LCC TX724.5.I4
 (ebook) | DDC 641.5954--dc23/eng/20220915
LC record available at https://lccn.loc.gov/2022043497
LC ebook record available at https://lccn.loc.gov/2022043498

Art direction and cover design by Morgan Krehbiel

Cover photo, author photo, and photos on pages viii, 5, 33, 68–69, 127–129 by Andrew Miller | Andrew Miller Photography

Photos on pages 46, 49, 67, 121, 123–124, 140 by Katherine Rasmussen Polovina | Luna Light Media

All other photos by Dave Monk and Gregg Lowe | Brave New Photos

Original food styling by Mary Valentin

Surrey Books is an imprint of Agate Publishing. Agate books are available in bulk at discount prices.
For more information, visit agatepublishing.com.

CONTENTS

ACKNOWLEDGMENTS

IT HAS TAKEN ME ALMOST TWO YEARS TO GET HERE. In that time, we went through a pandemic with everyone huddled at home. My older daughter applied for and left for college and my younger daughter skillfully navigated high school while playing club soccer. My husband ran his consulting business from our basement while all I did was cook. I honestly feel like I stood in my kitchen every single day for this entire period. I'm beyond exhausted!

From the outside it looks perfect. Mom constantly spewing out recipe after recipe while everyone comes down with outstretched arms, eager faces, and empty plates. It was nothing like that. I would try something, it would flop, and there would be a lot of frustrated screams—all from me. Often after a full day of recipe testing there still was nothing to eat for dinner. We'd order in and my girls would laughingly threaten to out me to all of you.

There were lentils everywhere. With three Instant Pots in various sizes cooking at one time, you often couldn't even see the countertops. Dinner was never easy because everything had to be logged before it could be eaten—the recipes had to be written down and photos needed to be taken. There were a lot of eye rolls and sighs.

Our freezer was so full that I had to take a shelf out and start stacking the food. That was even after I had created a group text begging friends to come over and pick up samples. Every time folks would show, I had to package things up, lock up our barky Australian Shepherd, and essentially disrupt the household.

I missed meetings with teachers, forgot doctors' appointments, and had to say no to just plain hanging out. And for this, I want to thank my family. They may not have always liked what I needed to do to get this book done, but they have been there from the beginning cheering. So, to my husband, Sandeep, my older daughter, Neha, and my younger daughter, Aria, thank you from the bottom of my heart. I cannot do this without you because I do it for you. It's my gift to you.

Sandeep, your constant complaining that the food was so good that you couldn't stop eating—well, that was quite the compliment! It says it all. We've built something wonderful at home. I'm proud that we are doing this together and that our mutual motto is to just put our heads down and work. You are one of the hardest workers I know, and I use you as my example every day.

Neha, you truly are one of the best editors I've ever worked with. You patiently read over my final manuscript while you were home on winter break from Northwestern University. Your edits made this book tighter and so much better. You always make me so proud! And, most importantly, you make me better. I know I am your mom, so why is it that I am always learning from you? You will always be my old soul packaged so beautifully.

Aria, thank you for the constant feedback on all my recipes. You were the one that suggested I prep three versions of one recipe at a time in different sizes so I could knock them all out in one day. You would come down to the kitchen and stir the pot, taste, and make recommendations on more spice, more cook time, or less water. You read and helped me edit recipes and sections of this book and gave me valuable advice along the way. You, my love, have such a future in food. When the recipes worked, oh the smiles! When they didn't? Let's not talk about that!

I'd be remiss if I didn't thank our crazy dog, Oliver, who would sit under my desk in my office for hours during the day as I typed away. He even loves lentils now. We have a lifetime supply in the freezer, so that's a good thing!

A huge thank you to all my recipe testers and food tasters. The first group took my recipes and made them verbatim in their own Instant Pots. The feedback was essential to this book. It was helpful to hear how much they loved the recipes—just reinforcing what I already knew: that flavor is key. But also, the small tips that helped along the way. One user told me how she appreciated me telling her to remove the trivet with tongs, another said it helped to tell her when she should press the CANCEL button, and still another said it was great that the techniques prevented any BURN warnings in his cooking. And so many of you were too scared to even open your Instant Pot boxes before we started this testing process. Congratulations to all of you! We have collectively come a long way.

To my tasters, thank you for picking up food always. My most eager was Charlotte. You were truly the best, most dedicated eater in the family. And I say family because I feel like you are. Every time you would come and pick up those big bags of food we would chat about our kids, life, and politics. Thank you for those conversations—they literally kept me sane during the crazy times. I began my food chats with Andy on the soccer pitch and I feel like through him we began our own conversations. I'll always be here to cook for you if you keep eating!

Many thanks to the brilliant photographers who made this book what it is: Andrew Miller with Andrew Miller Photography, Katherine Rasmussen Polovina with Luna Light Media, and Dave Monk and Gregg Lowe with Brave New Pictures. Thanks to Wendy Woodside of Wendycityfaces for makeup and the illustrious Sayuri with Charles Ifergan Salon for her flair with short hair—I wouldn't trust anyone else. And a huge thanks to Mary Valentin for the original food styling. Thank you to my assistant Patti Merendo for keeping me on track week after week as she had to listen to all my woes and excuses for missing our personal deadlines. We still got it done!

My sincerest thanks goes to team Agate for not only taking on this project enthusiastically, but taking my handwritten drawings of a chart-like recipe structure and replicating it perfectly. Amanda Gibson, Jane Seibold, Mira Green, Morgan Krehbiel, and Jacqueline Jarik, you are all rockstars. Without your patience, detailed editing, and sense of balance and graphic design my ideas could not have been replicated this beautifully.

As always, my sincerest thanks go to my publisher, Doug. I know this project was a bit of a question mark in the beginning. Why write just another Instant Pot cookbook? I truly appreciate that you listened to why I thought this would be different and trusted me to execute my vision. Now, let's sell some books!

INTRODUCTION

FEAR PREVENTED ME FROM WRITING THIS BOOK. There, I admitted it. As someone who takes pride in fearlessly attacking all my life obstacles, this is not an easy one to share. For years, I talked about writing this book, but every time I started, I was struck with panic. It felt overwhelming, daunting, and impossible.

Maybe you've felt the same about using a pressure cooker? That's why I want to share my story with you. The irony is that in India pressure cookers are widely used. But they are typically a stovetop version that whistles during the cooking process. Once you get used to them, they are simple, but if you don't, then you'll likely be fearful as I was. Many of my Indian American friends who have been raised outside of India feel like they've missed the opportunity to get comfortable with this type of appliance.

When I was younger, I witnessed my mother's old-school stovetop pressure cooker blow up in our small apartment in Voorhees, New Jersey. We were cleaning yellow dal off the ceiling for months. She now says she doesn't quite remember that, but I'll never forget it. My mother, though she grew up in India where pressure cookers are used regularly, simply put the pressure cooker away for good and started using a slow cooker.

Then, in 2015, while on a book tour in South Carolina, an instructor showed me her new electric pressure cooker. Instead of the stove, it was powered by plugging into an outlet. It was not only easy to use, but incredibly safe. It was in that moment I realized this would be the way many of us who had a fear of stovetop pressure cookers could overcome our inhibitions.

But it seemed I waited too long. The Instant Pot craze hit the American market in 2010 and so did many Indian cookbooks that used it. What a perfect name—at the perfect time—for the perfect appliance! It took off. My fear was replaced with deep personal disappointment that I had missed my opportunity.

That is, until all of you stepped in! I started to hear from fans everywhere, especially those of you who use my first book, *The Indian Slow Cooker*. Many wanted to know why I had not written a pressure cooker book. And so many were already translating my slow cooker recipes to the Instant Pot. I took it as a sign.

I realized that *The Indian Slow Cooker*, when it released in 2010, was a runaway success for a variety of reasons. The most obvious was that it used an appliance most Americans were familiar with—a slow cooker.

But it also offered the perfect array of recipes. If you only made the recipes in that book over the course of a year, your family would be impressed with your variety of Indian cuisine. This is true even if you are Indian. It's filled with traditional, delicious homestyle dishes that we grew up eating. Sure, there is always more to make and learn, but these are the basics—the essentials. And it's all there in one book.

There's also deep flavor. I take pride in delivering a high level of taste and authentic seasoning. It's something that we demand in our family. Both my husband and I come from families from small villages in the heart of Punjab. We love fiery curries and deep, complex taste profiles that our region is known for, and we won't settle.

I wanted to also offer something that other Indian Instant Pot books don't—tested recipes for a variety of Instant Pot sizes. Many books offer one recipe for, say, 1 cup of beans. For our family of four, we typically need to double or triple that. But how do I successfully do that? Scaling up and down is not always a straight path in the world of recipe testing. So, I embarked on this project with the goal to write three books in one. Every single recipe has been perfected such that it can be made in a 3-, 6-, and 8-quart pressure cooker successfully. This meant testing each recipe dozens of times. And they are arranged in a chart so you can easily reference and cross-reference the ingredients, cook times, and yields.

As I scaled recipes, I realized that some Indian recipes made successfully in a small pressure cooker often give you a burn warning once made in a larger vessel. I noticed that users of other cookbooks complained about this as well. So, I had to test that much more to make sure they all worked perfectly no matter how much or how little you wanted to make.

I am grateful that my publisher listened to my thoughts and gave me the creative bandwidth to run with this project. I'm truly so proud of the work that I've put into this book. The recipes are delicious, practical, and useful.

The one thing that I insisted on with every recipe in this book is authentic flavor, which is why testing took so much time. I would not stop until my family tasted no difference between the dishes coming from the Instant Pot and those that I cooked in the slow cooker and on the stovetop. I nailed it, but it took me over a year to truly lock in all that flavor for which my recipes and my platform *Indian As Apple Pie* are known. My daughter Aria sat me down after over a year of complaining about the food from the Instant Pot to tell me, "Mom, I think you did it." Meaning that the food I was creating was rock solid and that now she was enjoying the Indian food from our Instant Pot. What an endorsement from my girl who has grown up with my cooking, my cookbooks, and a very high bar when it comes to Indian cuisine!

Everything I create leads with flavor. My parents moved to America when I was three, and after a series of moves, we ended up in King of Prussia, Pennsylvania. Growing up, I ate Indian food daily. I spent many summers in India, watching my paternal grandmother and others in her village make many of the recipes in this book. There, they mash spices by hand and toil over hot clay stoves for hours at a time. They also use pressure cookers, which are fast but often intimidating.

As a former television reporter, writer, and now a small business owner, I just don't have the luxury of extra time in my day. That's why in all my books, and especially this one, I'm always determined to find ways to produce traditional Indian flavors without tons of work. But the flavor must be there.

Don't get me wrong, some slicing and dicing are still involved in these recipes. But, with the right tools, even those tasks are not complicated. You just need to know which spices and kitchen gadgets to have on hand. This book will spell it out for you.

Why bother making Indian food at home? Because homestyle Indian cuisine is incredibly healthy and healthy food is important to our community and beyond. The latest research shows that Asian Indians have one of the highest rates of heart disease in the world, possibly because of their genetic makeup. If you are of South Asian descent, you don't need a statistic for proof. All you likely need to do is look at your own family. In mine, I've lost three dear uncles to heart disease. My father and late father-in-law have fought this battle as well. My recipes offer oil-light, nonfat, even vegan options to the dinner table. Spicy, flavorful, and authentic cuisine doesn't have to be loaded with unhealthy oils and fats. My book will prove it to every person in your life that suffers from these illnesses. Spice is the perfect substitute for oils and fats and has natural healing properties.

There's variety in this book. I've offered you an extended chapter on legumes (beans, peas, and lentils) and chapters on vegetables, meats, and desserts. Your family will love the flavor, and you can always modify the level of heat and salt according to taste preference.

There is nothing healthier than beans, lentils, and peas. Add the flavor of authentic spices like cumin and turmeric to the health benefits, and you have recipes that you'll make for years to come. My recipes are all based on traditional family recipes that have been handed down through the generations—from my grandparents to my own parents and now from me to my two girls and to you.

As I say in every book that I write, "Welcome to the Family!" I'm so grateful that it keeps on growing and that you are a part of it.

1

GETTING STARTED

"The advantage of Indian pressure cooking is that it is scalable. . . . Virtually every recipe can be doubled, or cut in half or by a third, and with a few tweaks its taste and look will parallel the original recipe."

What in the World Is a Pressure Cooker vs. an Instant Pot vs. a Multicooker vs. an Electric Pressure Cooker? Why Should I Use One?

It's crazy to me that with all the Instant Pot cookbooks out there, there is still so much confusion. It hit me at a party a few years back. My friends (most of whom were Indian American) bombarded me with questions about the Instant Pot. They already cooked with a traditional stovetop pressure cooker and did not understand why folks raved over the Instant Pot. They wondered if they needed to invest in another kitchen appliance. My answer was, "It depends."

The pressure cooker seems novel, but it has been around for quite some time. Its forerunner, called the "Steam Digester," was invented in 1679 by the French-born physicist Denis Papin. It was a sealed pot that forced the temperature inside to as high as 266 degrees Fahrenheit, increasing the boiling point of water to cook foods faster. The higher temperature cut cook times dramatically.

It wasn't until the late 1940s that various companies began developing pressure cookers for the home cook. The use of pressure cookers began steadily growing through the '60s and '70s, more so in Asia and Europe, and somewhat in America. In the 1990s companies began offering digital pressure cookers and ones that were electric, no longer needing a stove to operate. The consumer demand for these appliances began to grow in North America as the focus on fast, healthy eating and cooking at home began to steadily increase. These electric versions were also safer.

In early 2000, a group of Canadian designers began developing a "new age" electric pressure cooker that prioritized safety; cooked beans, meat, and vegetables to perfection; and would also serve as a slow cooker, rice cooker, steamer, sauté pan, yogurt maker, and warmer. This multicooker did not need to be watched because it did not use a stove to operate. In 2010 the first Instant Pot was introduced. The "Instant Pot" was the brand name for what was an electric multicooker—essentially, a pressure cooker that did the work of seven or more different appliances.

The built-in safety features and brilliant name are what have helped elevate the Instant Pot's popularity. There are eleven safety mechanisms, including temperature monitoring to avoid burning food, a safety lid lock to prevent an accidental opening of the lid when the device is pressurized, and an anti-blockage vent that prevents food debris from blocking the vent, to name just a few. These safety measures were music to the ears of scaredy-cats like me when it came to pressure cooking. It made the idea of using one something everyone could achieve. This should be music to your ears as well if yours is still in a box.

So, what exactly is a pressure cooker again? Simply put, it's a device that cooks food by building heat and pressure inside a pot fitted with a lid that firmly seals steam inside. The temperature can max out at 250 degrees Fahrenheit depending on the pressure cooker type and model. This high heat cooks food faster than other cooking methods. Pressure cookers can be heated in different ways. Some operate on a stove. Others operate with electricity and come with a cord that simply plugs into the appliance on one end and an electrical outlet on the other. Many of these electric pressure cookers now offer additional functions, making them "super" pressure cookers or multicookers—with functions that enable them to function like slow cookers, rice cookers, and yogurt makers—all in the same pot and with the push of a few buttons on a digital panel. There are many brands out there. Instant Pot is one of the most popular.

Is the Instant Pot magic? I get this question all the time. Along with, "If I buy an Instant Pot, will it make food instantly?" No. I am sorry to burst your bubble, but nothing is magic—not even takeout. Nor is it instant, no matter its name and how well it is marketed. Generally, stovetop and electric pressure cookers will cut your cook time by up to 50 percent. The reason I emphasize that it's not magic is because to work, regardless of the heat source (stove or electrical), a pressure cooker must first build pressure. And, once a dish is cooked, the pressure must be released completely to safely open the lid. So, say you have beans that will cook in 30 minutes. Your pressure cooker will take about 20 minutes to build pressure or "warm up" and then 20 minutes to release pressure or "cool down." That is a total of 1 hour 10 minutes, including the cook time. That's faster than other methods, but it's not instant.

But don't lose hope. There is some magic. An electric pressure cooker helps with workflow. You can literally walk away during the warm-up, cook, and cool-down times. Once the pot is closed most of that time is hands off—you can go about your chores and the Instant Pot will do the work for you. That's in essence the brilliance of the Instant Pot and electric pressure cookers. There are some exceptions—like in my chapter on Vegetables, but it's still generally much easier to leave things to cook and cool down with a simple press of a button than to keep an eye on something that could burn on a stove.

A pressure cooker (stovetop and electric) also gives you a deeper level of flavor than some stovetop cooking. Though, I will argue that it does not always match the flavor of slow cooking. I worked diligently to replicate my family's high standard of Indian flavors in the Instant Pot.

What size Instant Pot should I purchase? The size of Instant Pot or electric pressure cooker you need depends on how much storage space you have in your kitchen, how much product you and your family eat, and if you want leftovers. Most electric pressure cookers and multicookers come in a range of sizes from 3 to 9 quarts. But they do not hold as much product as you may think. When you look in the inner pot of your appliance, you'll see a mark that is usually called the PC MAX line, at the two-thirds fill point of the inner pot. You cannot safely operate your appliance if you fill it above this line. Why? Because you need room in your inner pot for the pressure to build safely. This is one of the biggest misconceptions about pressure cookers. Many users think that if they purchase a 6-quart Instant Pot they will be able to make 6 quarts of product. Nope. If you would like to make more, then you'll want to purchase a larger one. Also remember that you can make less product in a larger pot (if there is enough water), but you can't cram more product into a smaller pot. If you are going to purchase only one pot, then go for the 6-quart. However, I personally love my 3-quart as well for quick weekday dinners when I want just enough food to feed my family of four or when I want to make a batch of plain black beans or chickpeas like I showcase in Chapter 3. When cooking lentils and grains, the Instant Pot manual officially recommends filling the inner pot halfway. I tested all my recipes at least a dozen times (four times for each size), and many testers also tried them. They all worked. You can also follow the recipes for the legume section as written, but only fill the inner pot halfway with water. After cooking, add in the remaining amount of water and simmer.

Scaling recipes is generally straightforward. The cook time surprisingly remains the same (with very few exceptions), but what may change a bit are the warm-up and perhaps cool-down times (unless you are using a manual release). The reason why I tested all my recipes for the three most common sizes of pressure cookers is to make sure I logged the warm-up and cool-down times for you and ensured that I would not get a BURN warning as I scaled my recipes up. Recipes often worked in smaller sizes but needed to be tweaked to work in larger sizes.

I use my stovetop pressure cooker all the time—do I need to purchase another appliance?

The short answer is no—but you may want to at some point if you like the additional features of a multi-cooker/electric pressure cooker. If you already feel comfortable with a stovetop pressure cooker, congratulations! You've overcome the fear that still grips many of us. You can make any electric pressure cooker recipe in a stovetop pressure cooker, but keep one thing in mind. Stovetop pressure cookers get a few notches hotter than their electric counterparts. As a general guideline, when operating at full heat, a stovetop pressure cooker can get to about 250 degrees Fahrenheit versus an Instant Pot that gets to about 242 degrees Fahrenheit. When using a stovetop pressure cooker for my Instant Pot recipes, reduce the cook time by 5 to 10 minutes, possibly a little more. You can make all the recipes in this book in your stovetop pressure cooker with minimal tweaking. Just jot the cook times down for future reference.

Is the Instant Pot the only electric pressure cooker/multicooker on the market? No. There are
many fantastic brands out there, including ones made by Breville, Ninja, Cuisinart, Fagor, and Crockpot. Do your own research to understand and navigate the differences.

Which model Instant Pot should I purchase? It can be confusing because there are many different
models on the market now. The more recent ones even use wireless technology. Personally, I prefer to keep things as simple as possible. For this book, I used the Instant Pot Duo in the 3-, 6-, and 8-quart sizes. All my recipes can be used with other models, but you may need to tweak cook times and ingredient quantities. A few of my testers used different Instant Pot models and with just a few adjustments were successful. Always refer to the manual.

How are these Indian recipes in the Instant Pot different from others? My goal was to write an
Indian Instant Pot cookbook that gives you everything. Full, authentic Indian flavor, family-style portions, and recipes that work for any size Instant Pot. I have a freezer brimming with leftovers to prove that I've tried these recipes dozens upon dozens of times. I achieved full flavor by ramping up some spices and in some cases pulling back on the water added. My approach was to tackle this like a science project to consistently nail the flavor and consistency.

Now that I feel comfortable using my Instant Pot, should I get rid of all my other appliances, pots, and pans? NO! Someone told me they did this as they started to use their Instant Pot for everything, and I could only feel sad for them. I also did not believe them. Why in the world would you want one appliance for everything? No slow cooking? No more Le Creuset Dutch oven? No more stovetop cooking? My week would feel super bleak. I always like to say that no one day in my week is the same as another, so the way I cook also changes. While during the week I may reach for quick-cooking options, on the weekend I slow down and like trying other things that might take more time and precision in the kitchen. My point is, use your electric pressure cooker and/or Instant Pot to enhance your meals and your life, but don't let it take over. It may not make sense to make everything in an Instant Pot—or maybe for you it does. Variety is what keeps cooking and life interesting. There can be many ways to get to the same point. Do what is good for you and works for you and your family, and don't let anyone tell you different.

Now, let's get started!

Instant Pot Terms & Functions

Learning to use an Instant Pot (IP) or electric pressure cooker can initially feel like learning a new language. I promise it's much easier than it seems. But, like anything else, practice makes perfect. Here are some key terms that will help as you navigate. You don't need to memorize them. Just refer to this list as you start using the Instant Pot, and it eventually becomes intuitive.

- **OFF:** As soon as you plug in the Instant Pot, the display will flash the word OFF. This is your cue to select the pressure cook time and heat level. Once selected, after 10 seconds the IP will start. Need more time? Just press CANCEL and start over.

- **CANCEL:** This button is your friend and savior. No matter what you are doing, if you get nervous or feel like you've made a mistake, just hit this button, and start over. Also press it to switch functions in the middle of a recipe. Say you start with sauté and then want to pressure cook an item. Press the CANCEL button after the first step to program the second. All my recipes clearly state when to press CANCEL.

- **SAUTE (SIMMER & BROWNING):** This function only works with the lid off. There are three levels: LESS/NORMAL/MORE, which are LOW/MEDIUM/HIGH in some models. They correspond to the level of heat. LESS ranges from 275 to 302 degrees Fahrenheit; NORMAL ranges from 320 to 349 degrees Fahrenheit; and MORE ranges from 347 to 410 degrees Fahrenheit. These numbers are not set in stone, but they give you an idea of which level to pick. Most Indian *tarka* (oil-spice infusion, also spelled *tardka*) is conducted at the highest level to break down the spices. When gently cooking garlic and shallots for a soup, use the LOW setting. If you need to sear or brown your meat, go for MORE. When you press the SAUTE button, the number 30 will appear on the panel. This is simply for safety and ensures that the appliance will automatically turn off after 30 minutes of sautéing in case you forget about it. If you want to sauté for longer, simply press the SAUTE button again.

- **WARM UP:** This is the time it takes to build pressure. It automatically starts to calculate once you lock the lid into place and program the Instant Pot. It will beep to indicate the warm up has started. The reason I painstakingly calculated this time for every recipe is so that you know precisely how long it takes to make a dish. I found this time increases based on how much water and product is in the Instant Pot. So if you cook a larger batch of a recipe, no matter the size of the Instant Pot you use, be prepared for a longer warm-up time, though the cook time generally stays the same. While I used a stopwatch to calculate the time for every recipe, just know that there can be slight variations.

- **COOK:** This is the amount of time you program into the Instant Pot to cook an item. You can use pre-set buttons. All these buttons default to high pressure except for RICE, which defaults to low pressure. I prefer using the + and − buttons to enter the time myself to be more precise. If you prefer, you can use a pre-set button and then adjust the time up or down according to the recipe.

- **PRESSURE COOKING:** This function only works with the lid on and locked in place. This button starts your pressure-cooking process. When you press it, the last cook time will pop up—the Instant Pot has a digital memory! After 10 seconds, cooking will automatically start. There is no ENTER button. If you need more time or make a mistake, just press CANCEL.

- **PRESSURE LEVEL:** This is the button that determines the level of heat when you pressure cook. Press the button for LOW or HIGH. The ideal pressure level button is clearly indicated in my recipes.

- **COOL DOWN:** The type of cool down and time varies depending on the type of ingredients you are cooking and the recipe's desired consistency. Once the cooking is complete, you cannot just open the lid. There is still steam built up in the pot that must be safely released. You know it's safe to open the lid when the Instant Pot's metal float valve drops with a tiny click. You can leave the pressure cooker to cool down on its own, you can physically turn the valve to release the steam, or you can combine the two methods. The longer you allow the dish to sit in its own steam, the more it will cook. This is fine for some items like beans, but not for others like vegetables.

- **NATURAL RELEASE or NATURAL PRESSURE RELEASE (NR-NPR):** With this method, you do absolutely nothing after cooking is complete. The pressure slowly releases and then the float valve eventually drops. Allowing the steam to release on its own can take time (anywhere from 5 to 30 minutes or more), but if you are running errands, have plenty of time, and the ingredients will hold up, it's an easy and safe method to depressurize a pressure cooker. If a recipe states NR with no time indicated, that means you should let the steam release on its own until the float valve drops to indicate it's safe to open the lid.

- **MANUAL RELEASE or QUICK RELEASE (MR-QR):** These are two terms for the same thing. With this method, you physically move the pressure-release valve, so you depressurize the vessel faster. In my recipes I use the term MANUAL RELEASE because it reflects physically doing something. NEVER EVER place your hand over the pressure-release valve/vents. You will get burned—the steam is extremely hot. If you are nervous, use a set of tongs, a long-handled spoon, or a spatula to safely move the pressure-release valve to the desired position. If you are cooking a brothy soup or *dal*, place a dishcloth lightly over the pressure-release valve so the product inside does not splatter. Be sure to use one you don't mind staining.

- **KEEP WARM:** This function activates automatically at the end of cooking and keeps the food warm in the pot on a low temperature.

- **ELEVATED TRIVET COOKING:** This is my term for recipes that cannot touch the bottom of the inner pot when pressure cooking because there is a possibility they will burn. Simply use the metal trivet that comes with the Instant Pot. Many now have "wings" or handles so that once cooking is done, you can easily pull them out. If your trivet does not, just use a narrow set of tongs to get in there and grab an edge. Never use your bare hands. I use a trivet for many recipes in my Vegetables and Meat sections that require less water and use ingredients like tomato and tomato paste that could trigger a BURN warning.

- **SLING:** This is a "hammock" of sorts created from folded aluminum foil so that a pot can sit in the Instant Pot, cook, and then more easily be removed.

- **POT-IN-POT COOKING (PIP):** Use this method when cooking something that needs little to no moisture. Remember, a pressure cooker can only build steam if there is a certain amount of water/moisture in the pot. But some recipes, including desserts, would be ruined if you added water. By using a heatproof dish in the inner pot, you can add water to the bottom, position a trivet in the pot, and then place the heatproof dish on the trivet. Usually, the inner pot of a smaller pressure cooker works well as the heatproof dish. Just be sure you have enough clearance to close the lid. The only downside to this method is that the amount of product you make is limited by the size of the dish used to cook it in. If you know this when making a recipe, you'll be fine. And no BURN warning! This method is perfect for making something with a low-liquid content, steaming desserts, reheating food, or making multiple dishes at the same time.

- **SLOW COOK/YOGURT/SAUTE:** All three functions operate with the lid off. For these functions only, the pressure-release valve does *not* need to be in the closed or sealed position. For all other cooking it *must* be in the closed or sealed position.

This is the NEVER FORGET section. There are a few things that you never want to overlook when using an electric pressure cooker.

- Never forget the **SEALING RING**. This is the rubbery ring inside the lid that ensures steam does not leak during the cooking process. If it is loose or if you forget to put it in, you won't be able to pressure cook because the steam will escape. You can remove it and wash it in a dishwasher, but always return it. It's easy to fit into the crevice of the inner rim of the lid. No matter how much you wash it, this ring can retain smells. You can purchase an extra one to swap out for desserts or baking. Usually, the smell does not affect the taste of the ingredients that are cooking.

- Never forget the metal **INNER POT**. Sounds silly, but some users, in their rush to cook, place their ingredients in the Instant Pot base rather than in the inner pot. Never ever do this. It can compromise the mechanics of the Instant Pot.

- Never forget the **LIQUID**. A pressure cooker can only successfully build steam and pressure with an appropriate amount of liquid in the pot. The amount you need will depend on the type and size of pressure cooker you have, so read the instructions carefully. When making a smaller pressure cooker recipe in a larger model, be sure to increase the water appropriately. This was critical for recipes in my Vegetables section, where the minimal amount of water is used. The guidelines on how much water to use for each size Instant Pot has changed a bit over the years (from ¼ cup for a 3-quart IP to 1 cup and more for larger sizes). It can also depend on how much natural liquid is in your ingredients. This won't matter much for legumes, where you already use ample water. But when cooking Indian vegetable and meat dishes successfully you cannot add too much water. It just won't taste right, nor will it taste like Indian food. Follow the water recommendations in my recipes closely.

- Never forget to only cook with the steam valve in the **SEALING** position by turning it up and clockwise to the 11 o'clock position. If it is in the **VENTING** position it will release steam as you cook.

- Never forget to move your hand away from the holes that release the steam in the steam valve. Steam is extremely hot and can burn.

- Never forget that you do not need to panic—ever. The Instant Pot is equipped with safety mechanisms. If you get a **BURN** warning, be proactive. Wait a minute or two to see if it corrects itself, and if it does not, then press **CANCEL**, stir the contents, add more water, and start again. If the bottom of the inner pot is even slightly burned, remove the contents, clean out the inner pot, and start over. Keep in mind that when tomatoes and tomato paste touch the bottom of the inner pot and cook at high heat, they can burn. That's why in my Vegetables and Meat sections I encourage you to add them last and *not* stir the contents before cooking. If all else fails, dump all the ingredients into a pot and finish cooking on the stove. Remember, practice makes perfect.

How to Use This Book

YOU'LL NOTICE THAT THE FORMAT FOR THIS BOOK IS SLIGHTLY DIFFERENT FROM OTHERS. Each recipe has the precise cook times and ingredient quantities for three different sizes of the Instant Pot. Rather than give you this material as footnotes that can be cumbersome and confusing, each recipe is offered in color-coded columns. Each column corresponds to a different size Instant Pot. This way, you can easily and accurately zero in on the precise measurements when cooking. By offering detailed recipes for several sizes, I've taken the guesswork out of scaling recipes up or down. The instructions generally remain the same for all three sizes, but any slight variations are indicated.

Always remember that the recipes from a smaller Instant Pot can be made safely in a larger one as long as there is enough water, but you typically cannot make a larger recipe in a smaller pot. So a bean or lentil recipe showcased for the 3-quart version can be successfully made in the 6-quart or the 8-quart. When making dishes that require little to no water, as in the Vegetables section, just remember to increase the amount of water used according to the instructions for the larger Instant Pot. I like to emphasize this because I used the most product I could in any given Instant Pot size. So my smallest quantity of beans used is 2 cups rather than the 1 cup typical in most other recipes, which enables you to make the most of even your smallest Instant Pot. I truly hope this approach not only makes cooking simpler as you navigate different quantities of prepared foods, but that it also encourages you to use the Instant Pot for family dinners, parties, and larger gatherings with ease and precision in your kitchen and beyond.

Why Indian? Why Make It at Home?

WHEN YOU THINK OF COOKING INDIAN FOOD AT HOME, WHAT COMES TO MIND?
Be honest. If you are newer to Indian cuisine, it might be that you are concerned you'll have to invest in dozens upon dozens of unfamiliar spices. Or maybe it's that you'll be in the kitchen for hours preparing just one meal. Or that you'll need layer upon layer of cream and unhealthy oils, or—worse yet—that the food will be so incredibly spicy you won't be able to eat it?

If you already eat and appreciate Indian food, it may be butter chicken or *tikka masala* that comes to mind. Or a *dal makhani* or lamb *vindaloo*? But it stops there.

Don't worry, you are not alone. While Indian cuisine in the United States has certainly grown fans since I came out with my first cookbook in 2010, there is still educating to be done. Healthy Indian cuisine is a thing, and it can successfully be made at home. In fact, it's often even better when cooked at home—with the right ingredients and recipes.

While I love eating out in Indian restaurants, we do find the Indian food served and showcased to still be heavy with oil and cream. We just don't eat like that regularly. When I tell my friends that we eat Indian food just about every day, they are shocked because they often only know the food available in the mainstream Indian restaurants.

I hope that with this book and the ease of the Instant Pot, you will discover a whole new world of Indian cuisine that is at once fresh, healthy, and diverse. I also hope that if you are Indian and too busy to slow down to cook for your family regularly, this book will help you preserve your own Indian food memories and family recipes. I wish I'd had this book for myself when my girls were young and I worked the early shift as a reporter fighting for sleep and time.

If you still can't make the time to cook, share this book with your nanny, babysitter, or parent—whoever helps cook for your kids while you are working. They will be making Indian food the way you grew up eating it in no time. The recipes are so easy to follow, anyone can make them. And just like my first book, *The Indian Slow Cooker*, you can easily have healthy, nutritious Indian food waiting for you when you come home from a hard day of work. Or perhaps you have a caretaker for an elderly parent? Maybe the nursing home where they stay would like a recipe or two? Hand them a copy of this book. Every recipe can be tweaked at home for any dietary preference. If you don't want the heat? Take out the red chile powder and chile peppers. Want less or no salt? Simple. And so on. There is nothing that makes my aging parents happier than eating the foods they love, the way they made it themselves. Good food is the best therapy.

Indian spices, spice blends, legumes, and sauces are also easier than ever to find. To get the best taste profile, head to sources that you trust and ask a lot of questions. Better yet, find a local mom-and-pop Indian grocery store and support them. Or perhaps look for our grocery products through my website IndianAsApplePie.com. We have made it incredibly easy to source the right ingredients for the right recipe with one click.

How far we have come—how much further we'll go!

Indian Spices 101

MOST PEOPLE ARE AFRAID TO COOK INDIAN FOOD BECAUSE THEY MISTAKENLY BELIEVE that they need to have complicated spices on hand. I'm here to say "nonsense!" to that.

Yes, there are many spices out there. But to start cooking the Indian dishes most commonly found on restaurant menus, you only need a few key spices, some of which you may already have in your cupboard. To make most North Indian dishes, start by investing in cumin seeds, black or brown mustard seeds, ground coriander, turmeric powder, red chile powder, *kala namak* (black salt), and *garam masala*. I also like to keep regular table salt, kosher salt, and fine sea salt on hand for general flavoring.

All of the above spices can be found at any Indian grocery store. Most are also now available at well-stocked grocers like Whole Foods Market. If your local grocery store doesn't have the spices you need, then check on the internet. There are many online sites now that sell Indian spices including my own, IndianAsApplePie.com.

Storing and dispensing these spices will be incredibly simple if you invest in what's known among Indians as a *masala dabba*. This spice box is one of the quintessential tools in the Indian kitchen: a simple stainless steel box. Round in shape, it holds seven smaller bowls—small enough to fit into the palm of your hand—that hold small amounts of the seven essential spices needed for Indian cooking.

The best feature of this container is that the small bowls can be removed so that you can dole out spices right over any dish you are making. A tiny spoon inside the box helps get the measurements just right. The *dabba* can fit into most kitchen drawers and ensures that spices are readily available to add to oil as it heats up on the stovetop. Timing is essential to getting Indian food just right, and it's difficult to get the timing down if you are fumbling in cupboards and with various containers as you cook. If you purchase more than one *dabba*, each can be used to store the most-used spices for a particular region in India. You can even make one box for baking spices and another for Italian, or one for oatmeal toppings.

MASALA DABBA

1. Red Chile Powder
2. Ground Coriander
3. Black Mustard Seeds
4. Turmeric Powder
5. Black Salt/*Kala Namak*
6. *Garam Masala*
7. Cumin Seeds

The spices you use will vary depending on the region of India from which the dish originates. I am from Punjab, so much of what I've presented in this book is from North India, though I've also included some South Indian, Gujarati, and Goan recipes. Most Indian restaurants offer North Indian cuisine, so the dishes you're most used to eating, from *Palak Paneer* (see page 126) to Punjabi Chicken Curry (see page 139), are probably represented in this cookbook.

You will have the best luck cooking Indian food if you buy most of your spices whole and in small quantities. Ground, they have a shorter shelf life, so don't buy ground spices in large quantities unless you know you'll go through them quickly. I do purchase turmeric and red chile in powder form because it's difficult to grind these two spices. Red chile can irritate the eyes, and it's tough to find turmeric in its whole form.

Invest in a basic coffee grinder, and reserve it only for grinding whole spices. Grinding spices takes seconds. Put them in the grinder, push down for a few seconds, and they're ready to use. As long as the grinder stays dry, it only needs to be washed about once a month. An easy way to keep it fresh between uses is to add 1 teaspoon of raw, uncooked rice instead of spices. Turn the grinder on a few times. As it grinds the rice, any powders will also be collected. Dump the rice and presto—your grinder is nice and fresh without any washing!

Some recipes call for roasting spices. Don't be intimidated. Think of it as a way to get double duty from your spices. Use a dry, shallow pan—one that has no water in it or any remnants of oil. Put your spice in the pan and heat on medium-low heat for a few minutes, until browned. Stay close by as the spice cooks and shake the pan a few times to ensure it doesn't burn. When the spice has browned, immediately transfer it to a room-temperature glass or metal container to cool for about 10 minutes. (I avoid plastic, especially with hot ingredients.) If you grind roasted spices while they are hot, they will release moisture and may cake at the bottom of your grinder. If this happens, just scrape out your spice and add to your dish.

The key to keeping your spices fresh is to keep moisture away from the box in which you store your spices. The spoon you use to dispense the spices should be kept dry and clean. If you wash your containers, make sure they are completely dry before you refill them. And never use a spoon that was used for something else before but now looks dry. Spices are sensitive to contamination and you want to be as cautious as possible.

Ideally, store your spices in glass or metal containers. The essential oils in some spices can be powerful enough to eat through or melt plastic!

Below is a list of the spices used in all of the recipes in this book with a brief explanation on the taste of each and why it's used. Start slow, with the most basic and essential spices—you can always add more later.

Amla: This tiny fruit is an Indian gooseberry, which is extremely tart and the richest natural source of vitamin C. It's a delicious addition to one of my chickpea dishes (see page 84). Some soak *amla* in hot water and have it as a health drink in the morning. You'll find it at an Indian grocery store. I recommend buying it unsalted, dried, and sliced rather than shredded.

I'm proud to say most of the *amla* we use comes right from my mom's childhood home in Chandigarh, India. There is one tree in the backyard that gives off so much fruit that my aunt distributes it to visiting family members.

Asafoetida powder (*hing*): This is not the most pleasant-smelling ingredient, but it helps digestion when it is added to food in very small pinches. The smell is quite strong, so store it in an airtight, sealed container so the smell doesn't permeate the entire cupboard. One way to eliminate the smell is to put it in heated oil, butter, or *ghee*.

Bay leaf (Indian cassia leaves or *tej patta*): Indian bay leaves look like their European counterpart, but they have more of a cinnamon flavor and typically have three veins running down the leaves versus just one. You can find them in most Indian grocery stores, but if you don't have them, you can substitute European bay leaves.

Big/black cardamom (*badi elaichi*): This is a big, dark, woody version of the small, green cardamom we are all used to seeing. It tastes fantastic in my black chickpea curry. It's also a healer when you have a cold. Just crush it gently and add it into the boiling water when you make *chai*, and you should be on your way to feeling better. It tastes great in rice *palau* as well. It looks and tastes different than green cardamom, which is more floral, but both come from the same plant family.

Black salt (*kala namak*): This is my favorite Indian spice. It's actually a rock salt that's somewhat pinkish in color. It's called black salt because when wet, it darkens and looks slightly black. It has a tangy taste and smell and enhances the taste of any dish in which you use it. In North India, it is used to flavor snacks, salads, and yogurt. A little of this spice goes a long way, so be careful to use small amounts until you get the spicing just right.

Caraway seeds (*shyah jeera*): *Shyah* means black, and the reference to *jeera* is because caraway looks like cumin seeds. It adds a special flavor to certain Mughlai dishes (Pakistani and Indian cuisine influenced by the imperial kitchens of the Mughal Empire) and to my dry black chickpea curry (see page 88).

Cardamom (green and white) (*hari elaichi*): Cardamom is the flavor behind Indian tea and many other dishes, including well-spiced basmati rice, meat stews, and desserts such as *Kheer* (see page 162). The seeds are ground to make cardamom powder and are a great addition to mango smoothies. Cardamom is also a great breath freshener. My mother carries whole pods around in her purse and pulls some out to chew on after eating strong Indian food or raw onions. The green ones are most common in Indian cooking. The white, used in Europe for baking, is merely a green cardamom pod bleached white with sulfur dioxide.

Carom seeds (*ajwain, ajowan*): This small seed has a very pungent flavor and smell. It looks like cumin (*jeera*) and is used in Indian breads like *parantha* and in snacks. I use a pinch of it in the *kitchari*, as it has healing properties for an upset stomach. Take a teaspoon in hot water with a pinch of salt, and usually your stomachache will disappear.

CINNAMON STICKS

Cinnamon sticks (*dalchini*): In Indian cuisine, cinnamon is not reserved for baking but is included in many savory dishes, vegetarian and meat based. The best way to incorporate it into your food is to sauté a stick or two in hot oil or *ghee* to help pull out as much flavor as possible. Before eating your meal, pull out and discard the cinnamon sticks. You can also leave them in for flavor even when you refrigerate or reheat your dish. Just be sure your guests know to eat around them. A dash of ground cinnamon toward the end of cooking can also do the trick, but using the whole stick keeps the taste subtle, the way we prefer.

Cloves (*laung*): Small and black with a bumpy end, this tiny spice packs a strong punch. It's used to spice tea, basmati rice, and many other dishes. Use sparingly, as too much flavor can overpower a dish. Cloves are also used to cure toothaches. Just bite down on one in the area of the ache until the pain subsides.

Coriander seeds/powder (*sabud dhaniya*): Coriander is also known as cilantro. The seeds are round and yellow-green and come from the flowers of the coriander plant. My mother rarely used coriander powder in her cooking, but I've since realized its value in many dishes. It imparts a subtle, unique, lemony flavor. It also imparts more depth to a dish when used along with cumin seeds. Powdered coriander is available in most Indian grocery stores, but the freshest way to get the powder is to grind the seeds in a coffee grinder reserved for spices on an as-needed basis.

Cumin seeds (*jeera*): In North Indian cooking, *jeera* is an essential spice. The seeds smell earthy when heated in oil and impart a strong, characteristically North Indian flavor when used in curries, dried dishes, and rice.

Cumin, roasted: This is one of the best-kept secrets in the Indian kitchen. Roasted cumin is essential in most Indian snack foods, yogurt *raitas*, and many other dishes. It's easy to make as well. Just heat a dry pan over medium-high on the stovetop. Place about a tablespoon of cumin seeds in the pan and heat until they turn dark brown, almost black. Be careful not to burn them. Cool and then grind in a coffee grinder reserved for spices, in a mortar and pestle, or with a rolling pin between two paper towels.

Cumin and coriander seeds, roasted: This is a wonderful combination of the nuttier cumin and the lemon-flavored coriander. Mix one tablespoon of each seed in a shallow, dry pan on the stovetop over medium-high heat, and brown, but don't burn. Cool completely and then grind in a coffee grinder reserved for spices or in a mortar and pestle.

Curry leaves: If you haven't had the pleasure of trying curry leaves in your food, you really are missing out. These small, green leaves come from a tree native to India and Sri Lanka and are used predominantly in South Indian cooking. Typically, the leaves are roasted in oil and then added to a dish. Curry leaves are the essential ingredient in *Sambhar,* a South Indian stew (see page 70).

Fennel seeds (*saunf*): Great for digestion, these little green seeds with a licorice-type taste are usually found at the entrance of most Indian restaurants, to be eaten after a meal in small pinches for digestion and freshening the breath. I was excited to find a few dishes that incorporate the seeds fresh and roasted. I also like to include a pinch in my *masala* when making Indian tea. When boiled a few minutes in water, fennel seeds can relieve gas. When my girls were babies I would let them sip cooled spoonfuls of fennel water to help their tummies.

Fenugreek seeds/leaves (*methi* seeds/leaves): Technically a legume, fenugreek seeds are used as a spice in Indian cooking. They are small, hard, and mustard yellow in color with a distinct, bitter taste profile. This bitterness is usually welcome in the dishes in which they are used, such as *Kadhi* (see page 135) and Spicy Butternut Squash (see page 125). The key when using these seeds is to cook them just until they have browned. Too much cooking tends to enhance their bitterness.

The green leaves are delicious when used to make Indian breads such as *parantha* and dishes such as chicken curry (see page 139). They can be purchased fresh or dried. I prefer dried, because they are easier to find and impart a richer flavor. Crush them gently in your hand to release their flavor.

CURRY LEAVES

CUMIN SEEDS

GROUND CUMIN

ROASTED GROUND CUMIN

FENUGREEK SEEDS

CLOVES

CORIANDER SEEDS

GROUND CORIANDER

BLACK MUSTARD SEEDS

TURMERIC POWDER

BLACK SALT/*KALA NAMAK*

GARAM MASALA

GREEN CARDAMOM

Kokum (*cocum, kokam*): This small, round fruit is native to the western coastal region of Southern India. It's black to dark purple and has a seed inside. The meat is used to add a bit of depth and a unique sweet and salty taste to Indian dishes.

Mango powder (*amchur*): This is a tart, beige powder made from uncooked, dried green mangoes. It is wonderful sprinkled on Indian snack foods and in dishes such as okra, *karela* (bitter gourd), and fried potato. It takes the place of lemon juice or vinegar and is usually used at the end of the cooking process. It's also used to tenderize meat. It enhances the flavor profile of my red kidney bean curry or *Rajmah* (see page 79).

Masala: *Masala* is a mixture of spices—dry or wet. Most often, it refers to a mix of spices that are roasted and then ground down, like *garam masala* or *chana masala*, and are specific to certain dishes. A wet *masala* is like a soup starter and combines spices with other ingredients, including onion, ginger, and garlic, to create a base for many Indian curries. There are many dry spice *masalas* on the market. You can buy them pre-roasted and ground, or you can purchase whole spices and replicate the blends yourself. Referring to a spice blend used to cook Indian food as "curry" is a misnomer. We don't use a blend called curry to make our food, we use *masalas*. We refer to our dishes that have gravy as curries or by their specific names. In our cuisine, curry has little to do with spices and everything to do with the consistency of the dish, hence why a dry, spiced dish is not referred to as a curry.

- **Garam masala:** This spice mix is one of the most common in North India. It includes coriander, cumin, cloves, cardamom, black pepper, cinnamon, and nutmeg. You can purchase the spices already ground or buy a packet of all of the above combined but left whole for you to grind later. If you grind them yourself, remember to balance the amount of each spice used. And be careful, as the whole cinnamon can be a little challenging to grind all the way down. Don't be intimidated to go this route though—I've done it and the results are wonderful. In most dishes, the *garam masala* is sprinkled over the food toward the end of cooking, but I prefer to put it in at the beginning along with the other spices.

- **Chana masala:** This spice blend, found at any Indian grocer, has a unique tartness that is essential to my curried chickpea dish. Pomegranate, fenugreek, mustard, and coriander seeds are just a few of the key ingredients.

- **Chaat masala:** This spice mix is tart and ready to use for seasoning snacks called *chaats*. The spices that make this mix unique include asafoetida, *amchur* (green mango powder), black salt, cayenne, *ajwain*, cumin, and pepper. *Chaat masala* sprinkled on fruit or veggies enhances their taste and makes a great snack.

- *Sambhar* **powder:** This is an amazingly fragrant mix of spices that is used to spice a traditional South Indian lentil stew called *Sambhar* (see page 70). The stew is then eaten with *idli* or savory crepes called *dosas*. The spice blend includes legumes, curry leaves, dried chiles, *chana dal*, coriander seeds, cumin seeds, fenugreek seeds, mustard seeds, white poppy seeds, cinnamon sticks, and oil. See page 71 for the spice blend recipe.

Mustard seeds (*rai*): These seeds are to South India what cumin seeds are to North India. They come in yellow and brownish black. The brownish-black seeds are more commonly used in Indian cooking. The best way to cook with them is to put them into hot oil and then cover the pan until they pop a bit. Mustard seeds can be used in everything from salads, to lentil stews, to pickles. They can add tartness to a dish when ground to a powder, and they provide a mustard taste when ground to a paste.

Nigella seeds (*kalonji*): These small black seeds have the combined flavor of onions and black peppers. They are used in North India in pickles and as a decoration for breads such as *naan*.

Red chile powder (*lal mirch*): This red powder made from dried chiles adds color and heat to a dish. Use sparingly for a milder dish, but if you don't mind spicy food, you'll want to be more generous. Cayenne pepper is an acceptable substitute.

Saffron (*kesar*): For decades, saffron was the world's most expensive spice by weight. It's derived from the red dried stigma of the saffron crocus flower. A little goes a long way, and its musky taste adds depth to savory dishes such as *palau* and sweet dishes such as *Kheer* (see page 162). It's also used for prayer ceremonies and to make a red mark on the forehead as a blessing.

Tamarind (*imlee/imli*): Tamarind trees are easy to spot, with long, beige fruit hanging from their branches. The pods are used to make tamarind, a souring agent used in many Indian dishes, especially those common to South Indian cuisine. Tamarind, a legume, can be purchased as a block of pulp, which then needs to be boiled down and strained, or as tamarind puree or concentrate.

Turmeric powder (*haldi*): I love *haldi* because it's such a versatile spice. In its whole form, it looks a lot like ginger (both are rhizomes), but it's orange/yellow in color on the inside. In my mother's childhood home, they grow it in the backyard, dry it, and grind it into a powder, which they distribute among our large family.

Powdered *haldi* is critical to most Indian dishes. It's also an amazing healer. I add it to hot water with a black tea bag and salt and gargle with the combo to get rid of congestions and coughs. Some studies now indicate the compound curcumin in this amazing spice may help to prevent the onset of Alzheimer's disease. True or not, you can't go wrong by including turmeric in your diet. When you cook with it, be careful not to use too much. A little goes a long way, and the taste can overwhelm a dish. The healing properties are better absorbed by our bodies when turmeric (powder or fresh) is combined with black pepper and a fat such as oil, *ghee*, or even milk.

White salt (*namak*): Indians are pretty salt obsessed, and for good reason. Salt is an amazing flavor enhancer and a key ingredient to really getting the spices in a dish to mix and work together. I typically cook with fine sea salt, which has a blend of natural minerals. If you don't think you'll need as much salt as I've suggested in a recipe, go ahead and err on the side of caution by adding half of what is listed—you can always add more salt later. Remember, unless otherwise specified, always use level teaspoons or tablespoons. Also note that I've given you the amount of salt needed to eat your dish paired with rice or bread. If you'll be eating a dish alone, then you'll want to reduce the salt slightly.

Tools of the Trade

LIKE GETTING SPICES JUST RIGHT, CERTAIN KITCHEN TOOLS MAKE COOKING INDIAN food—especially in an Instant Pot—easier. Some you absolutely need, and some you can do without for now but might want to add later.

Instant Pots in different sizes: If you are only going to get one size, then go for the 6-quart. If you have the option to add another, I recommend the 3-quart for daily cooking. It's perfect for feeding up to four people. The 8-quart is the perfect size for entertaining and large-batch cooking and freezing. I tested all the recipes in this book in all three sizes, so you'll never have to guess about ingredients or cook times. You can't even begin to imagine what our freezer looked like after this project!

Spice box (*masala dabba*): This traditionally round, stainless steel box comes with up to seven round bowls and small serving spoons. It is ideal for housing your most-used spices. Keep it in a kitchen drawer to pull out as needed. For North Indian cooking, the most important spices to have on hand include whole cumin, mustard and coriander seeds, turmeric powder, red chile powder, green mango powder, and *garam masala*.

Coffee grinder: This small gadget can usually be picked up for under twenty bucks and is worth every penny. It's vital if you plan to grind your own spices. Just be sure to reserve it only for spices and use another grinder for coffee.

Mortar and pestle: This traditional spice grinder requires more effort but is wonderful when you just need to coarsely crush a few spices. We pull it out when making *masala* for Indian tea or for grinding down roasted cumin for *raita* (yogurt).

Hand or immersion blender: One of the best investments I've ever made, this long-handled tool with a blade at the bottom enables you to blend and mix a dish without transferring it to another container. Cooked spinach and mustard greens become *saag* in seconds, and cooked peas are blended into soups even faster. You can blend right in the Instant Pot after pressure cooking. If you don't have an immersion blender, a regular blender will do, but you'll have to take food out of the Instant Pot to blend and then transfer it back.

Food processor: A regular or mini food processor is essential to grind ingredients such as garlic, ginger, onion, and tomatoes.

Microplane grater: I have grown to rely on my tiny Microplane grater. When I conduct cooking demonstrations, I actually keep it in my back pocket. With it, I can quickly grate ginger and garlic instead of chopping it, and I can work on my cutting board or over my Instant Pot.

Electric kettle: Whenever I need hot, boiling water, I reach for my electric kettle. While you should not add boiling water to an Instant Pot or pressure cooker for cooking, I do use boiled, hot water to soak my legumes ahead of cooking. It speeds up the process and cuts my soak time to 1 hour, versus 6 hours to overnight in room temperature water.

Serrated peeler: You have a peeler, but how about a serrated one? It's simply heaven! With the ease of a regular peeler you can now peel tomatoes, peaches, and plums in seconds. No more boiling, roasting, or freezing your tomatoes to get the peel off!

Fresh Ingredients & Pantry Staples

Aata (roti/parantha flour): Indians favor this flour, found in Indian grocery stores, for making Indian flat breads such as *roti* and *parantha*. Traditionally, *aata* is made from whole durum wheat rather than the hard red variety that is commonly grown and used in the West. My mother still remembers her own mother sending out wheat kernels to be ground and used in the kitchen. The wheat used in India is lighter in color and softer than the variety used to make the flour found in most Western supermarkets. Over the years, *aata* sold by Indian grocers became a mixture of white and whole-wheat flour. It made for a lighter, fluffier *roti*, but also one that was less healthy. To get the most nutritional benefit out of your homemade Indian bread, purchase *aata* with a label that reads "100 percent whole wheat." If you don't have access to an Indian grocer, any whole-wheat flour will do the trick if combined with an equal amount of all-purpose flour. You can also substitute whole soft white wheat flour, now found in many baking aisles.

Achaar (Indian pickle): Indians adore their pickles, which are nothing like pickles found in the West. Indians pickle everything from mangoes and lemons to large red chile peppers. The fruits and vegetables are preserved in vinegar, brine, or their own juice. The taste can be sweet, spicy, sour, or a combination. These pickles are served on the sides of dishes and eaten in small bites along with bread or rice. The simplest meals sometimes consist of a stack of *rotis* and a delicious piece of *achaar* on the side.

Buttermilk: In many parts of India, buttermilk is eaten after meals in place of yogurt. A by-product of the butter-making process, it's easier to digest and has a delicious, tangy taste. Some use it to also make *paneer*.

Chile peppers: Using chiles in Indian cooking is not just about adding heat. It's also about adding flavor. Different chiles impart different tastes, and some work better than others in Indian cooking. The smaller the chile, the hotter it's likely to be and the more flavor it will have. The ideal chiles for Indian cooking are the small, fresh Thai chiles or the slightly longer serranos, which look like long, knobby fingers. The cayenne chile pepper is also a good choice. Avoid the jalapeño pepper because it has a very thick skin that just doesn't work well in Indian cooking. If that's all you can find, go ahead and use it, but be aware that it's not the best choice.

Also remember that most of a chile's heat is found in its seeds and membrane. If you want the flavor minus the heat, just cut out and discard both. Or, use whole chiles in your cooking, just cutting the stems away. This way, you get the amazing flavors without too much spice. The more you chop a chile, the more heat you release. Keep that in mind when deciding how many chiles to put into a dish. If you're using bigger, longer chiles you'll want to cut down on the number until you're used to the spiciness. In all my recipes, I've used the Thai chile, but I've provided a range on the number of chiles each recipe requires to suit our family's taste buds. Thus, if you are using a longer, bigger chile, use the smaller number listed. I also refer to chile with an "e" at the end to make a differentiation with chili with an "i," which often refers to a spicy stew or a Mexican/Tex-Mex spice blend.

Cilantro (_dhania_): This green, flavorful herb is absolutely essential to Indian cooking. Usually added at the end of cooking, it adds another dimension to the taste of your food. It's optional, but if you use it you can take a dish from perfect to heavenly. It's important to use this ingredient fresh. It can be found in all supermarkets now, especially because it's also commonly used in Mexican cooking. Use the stems along with the leaves.

Coconut: Shredded coconut is used in many Indian dishes and desserts. Ideally, it's best to shred the meat from a fresh coconut, but when fresh is not available, purchase it dried from the store. Most grocery stores carry shredded, unsweetened coconut. Avoid the shredded, sweetened coconut used for baking. The ideal coconut is frozen shredded, now found in many ethnic grocery stores and some mainstream grocers.

Coconut milk: If you've ever seen a young, fresh coconut split, you know that they contain a natural liquid. This liquid is not the milk. The milk is the white liquid derived from taking the grated white meat of a more mature coconut, mixing it with hot water, and squeezing it through cheesecloth. The smooth liquid that is squeezed out during this process is coconut milk. It is used extensively in regions in India where coconuts are commonly grown, like the southwest coast and Goa. You can use canned coconut milk that is either regular or light in the recipes in this book that call for coconut milk.

Garlic (_lassan_): The power of garlic is amazing. Of course it's a key ingredient in Indian foods. It's also a healer. If you have a cold or a fever, just mince a clove of garlic and swallow with water. You'll be better in a matter of hours. Because I use so much garlic, I usually buy it already peeled from the supermarket. Just be sure to use it in a timely fashion, as it goes bad faster than whole heads that you have to peel. If you don't think you'll get to it all, just freeze it.

Ghee (clarified butter/oil): In India (especially North), *ghee*, or clarified butter, is commonly used in all aspects of cooking. It's prized for its ability to be heated to high temperatures without burning or breaking down, for its aromatic taste and smell, and for the fact that it does not need to be refrigerated. But *ghee* is not the only thing you can use. Many Indian cooks also use a variety of vegetable oils. When picking one, look for an oil with a high smoke point and a taste profile that suits the dish you are cooking.

Mustard oil is used in North and East India, while untoasted sesame and peanut oil is used in the west, and coconut oil is used in the south. These oils all have strong flavors, so experiment first and see what works best for you.

For an extra nutritional boost, add 1 tablespoon (15 mL) of flaxseed oil to any dish or a dash on a hot *roti* before serving for essential omega-3 and -6 fatty acids. Avoid cooking with this oil, as heat will destroy its healthy properties.

Ginger (*adarak*): Ginger, a rhizome, is commonly used in Indian cooking. The freshest is young ginger with very thin, almost pink skin. I've only found it this way a few times, so look for the more common, thicker-skinned variety. Adding ginger to your dishes adds a flavor and a pop to your food that you can't get any other way. I prefer grated ginger in my recipes, as it adds more flavor with fewer pieces to bite into later. Try peeling a large piece of ginger and freezing it, which makes grating easier.

Gram flour (*besan*): If you're serious about Indian cooking, this pale yellow flour is one that you'll want to keep handy. It's made from skinned, split, and ground black chickpeas. I use it in my *Kadhi* recipe (see page 135), and it's also used for the batter to make *pakoras* (fried dumplings). It is also used as a thickener and for making thin pancakes or crepes. You may be able to find *besan* in your local supermarket. If you can't find it made from black chickpeas, you can use ground chickpea flour, made usually from white chickpeas and found in many mainstream markets. You can also grind your own in a high-powered blender or Vitamix in the dry jug from dried, black chickpeas, either with the skin or without.

Mint (*pudina*): In North India, unlike other parts of the country, mint is not used a great deal in the dishes themselves, though one or two may include this herb. Mint is primarily ground with spices, sometimes including cilantro, to make a popular green chutney that's eaten along with meals, on many Indian snack foods, and as a sandwich spread. I grew up loving butter and mint chutney sandwiches. Though incredibly simple, you just can't beat the taste. Unlike cilantro, the stems of mint are not edible. Pull the leaves off and use them, and cither discard the stems or put them in water so they grow roots and regenerate. Mint plants are very easy to grow. Most Indian families have a patch of mint in the back to make fresh chutney.

Onions (*pyaz*): The story goes that I've been eating raw onions since I was three years old. I believe it, because my daughters are the same way: onion obsessed. I love onions. I eat them raw. I'm a true Punjabi Indian! Yellow and red onions work best when cooking Indian food. White onions are too sweet for cooking, but they work well in side salads. Onions are essential in most Indian dishes and salads. Once you cook a dish, always top it with a handful of chopped onions. Keep in mind, however, that some communities in India don't cook with onions, garlic, or ginger because of religious and dietary reasons.

Paneer: Homemade cheese is important to most Indian households—especially if they don't eat meat, as it's a great source of protein. *Paneer* has the consistency of solid ricotta cheese. *Paneer* can be found in many grocery stores these days, but it's also pretty easy to make (see page 128). If you want to avoid milk-based products, substitute cubed, firm tofu (baked is even better). It's lighter, but other than that it's hard to tell the difference.

Rice (*chawal*): Basmati is among the most coveted varieties of rice in the world. The word itself means "fragrance" in Sanskrit, which is appropriate. The kernels are long, slender, and almost perfumed. I can still smell the exact combination of rice and whole spices cooking in my childhood home before any big party. True basmati is largely grown in North India, around the city of Dehra Dun. These days, as people become more health conscious, there has been a move to eat the rice in its more original form, brown basmati, and other brown rice varieties.

Tomatoes: With Indian food, the key is to include just the right amount of tart to offset the spice. So, when you purchase tomatoes, forgo the overly ripe and overly sweet ones, or save them for your salad. I like to use plum tomatoes, which are the right size and taste for Indian cooking. Diced tomato is standard in Indian cooking, but my kids don't like biting into cooked tomatoes. I have started using pureed tomato and we prefer the smoother texture. Some suggest removing seeds to avoid bitterness before pureeing in a blender, but I don't bother. With Indian food and spices, likely you won't even notice it. Another way to puree tomatoes is to grate them by hand over the large holes of a box grater until you're only left with the skin, which can be discarded.

Yogurt (*dahi/dhai*): Unlike in the West, in India we eat savory or salty yogurt with meals and save the sweetened for dessert. We also make our own yogurt, which makes for a slightly thinner, more sour variety than that found in most grocery stores. Use whatever plain yogurt is available, but try to make it one day and you might realize how easy and rewarding the process is. Making yogurt in the Instant Pot is incredibly simple with my recipe (see page 161).

Legumes: Lentils, Beans, & Peas

LEGUMES ARE SIMPLY SEEDS THAT GROW WITHIN PODS. THEY COME IN MANY SHAPES and sizes and are a huge part of the Indian diet, acting as a high-protein, low-fat option for hundreds of thousands of vegetarians. Legumes are also high in fiber, folate, potassium, iron, magnesium, and phyto-chemicals—a group of compounds that may help prevent degenerative diseases such as cardiovascular disease and cancer.

Legumes include lentils, beans, and peas. I like to purchase mine dried rather than in cans because dried are not only cheaper, they also break down better during the cooking process. Canned beans and lentils are already saturated with liquid, so they won't absorb any cooking liquid and thus won't break down as well. This book will teach you how to cook dried legumes in just a few simple steps in an Instant Pot.

The variety of available beans and lentils, let alone the prospect of learning how to effectively cook each one, can be overwhelming. Some are better known by their English name and some by their Hindi counterpart, so I've tried to make identification as simple as possible. Each legume is listed by its English and Hindi names, including any alternative ways to refer to it. Keep in mind that most legumes can be purchased in four differ-ent forms:

1. The original, whole legume with the skin intact. Usually the word *sabut* or *sabud*, which means "whole" in Hindi, precedes the name of the legume to indicate that it is in its original form, with nothing removed. This is obviously the healthiest form of any legume, but it takes longer to cook because the skin is thicker and the legume has not been cut.

2. The whole legume without skin.

3. The split legume with the skin on (called *chilkha*, which means "skin" in Hindi).

4. The split legume with no skin (called *dhuli*, which means "washed" in Hindi).

Amazingly, the different forms of one type of lentil, bean, or pea—though they all start from the same source—can have strikingly different results when used in the same recipe. Cooking times will vary. Generally, anything with the skin on will take longer to cook but will also be more nutritious than its skinned and split counterpart.

Many of these legumes are also referred to by the generic term *dal* (also spelled *dahl*). I grew up in a Punjabi household, where *dals* referred to soupy lentils. But folks from other parts of India call soupy beans, dry lentils, dry beans, and even lentils cooked with rice *dals*. Don't let the term throw you off. And, when in doubt as to whether something is technically a lentil, bean, or pea, it's safe to call it a *dal*.

That said, a wonderful variety of legumes are now available in mainstream grocery stores, although they will be less expensive if you can find them at an Indian grocery store. Most members of the Indian community have a favorite Indian grocer they'll visit once a month or so to stock up on the basics. If you are going to make a habit of eating legumes, it makes sense to buy them in larger, cheaper quantities. I buy dried legumes in 4-pound bags. Buying online, including from my website, Indian As Apple Pie, is another great option.

Important! Regardless of where you purchase the legumes, it's a good idea to quickly sift through them before you use them or transfer them to another container. Often, bits of debris, small rocks, and other particles get mixed in with the product, and you'd never want a guest to chomp down on a piece of gravel. Never wash dried legumes until you're ready to cook, as storing them with any moisture can spoil the whole batch.

To sift through the lentils and beans, simply take a white plate (one with a pattern will distract the eye) and pour about 1 cup of the legumes on the side farthest away from you. Quickly bring small amounts of the product toward you with your hand. If you see any foreign particles and rocks simply pick them out and throw them away. Once I've sorted through them, I store the legumes in labeled glass containers I keep lined up on my pantry shelf.

When you are ready to cook them, put the dried legumes in a deep bowl. Cover them with water and scrub them clean with your hands. The water will look murky the first couple of times; just throw it away and repeat the process a few times with clean water.

At times you'll get a bad batch of legumes. If you find a powder at the bottom of the bag or tiny holes through the legumes, the batch may have been infested by insects. If this is the case, throw away the entire batch and start over. Remember, this is real, whole food and it happens.

Most legumes, once cooked, will keep for about three days in the refrigerator and for up to three months in the freezer. You can reheat them in the microwave or on the stovetop. I prefer the stove because it enables me to reconstitute the dish a bit. Usually, as they sit, legumes continue to absorb more water. So, don't be surprised when you pull a dish out of the refrigerator and find that it's thicker than when you put it in. All you have to do is add a little water and heat it slowly. Remember, you'll have to compensate for the diluted flavor by adding a bit more salt and maybe some red chile pepper.

The variety of beans and lentils out there is almost mind-blowing. I only list those that are most commonly used in Indian cooking. If you see another legume that looks interesting, bring it home and try it in one of the recipes listed in this book. You may just create your own favorite dish.

Black *dal*, black gram (*urad*, *maa*, *matpe* beans): This legume, technically a bean, is one of the best known throughout India, especially because of its use in many Hindu ceremonies. It's easy to recognize because it's jet-black, tiny, and oval shaped. Like other *dals*, it comes in four forms: whole with the skin on (*sabut urad*), whole with the skin off, split with the skin on (*urad dal*), and split with the skin off. Of course, the first form is the least processed. The other forms of this legume have their own unique textures and qualities when cooked. Removing the skin and splitting the *dal* makes it creamier and easier to digest. While technically a bean, I don't refer to it as such so it's not confused with the black beans typically used in Mexican cooking.

Brown lentils (*masoor*, *masar*, *mussoor*): These dark, round, disc-like true lentils are usually sold and used skinned and split. In this form, they are almost salmon in color and better known in the West as "red lentils" or *masoor dal*. A bit bizarre, but when cooked they turn yellow. They cook quickly and make a very easy meal when you're short on time.

Cowpeas, black-eyed peas/beans (*lobia*, *rongi*), and red cowpeas (*sabut chowli*): When you think of black-eyed peas, cooking from the Southern region of the United States usually comes to mind: simple comfort food. It makes sense, as these beans originated in Africa. Black-eyed peas are white or beige in color with a black spot in the middle. Red cowpeas are reddish brown in color, with an oval shape and a black spot in the middle. Both varieties make a great Indian curry, with their earthy, filling taste, and are especially good when mixed with greens or coconut milk.

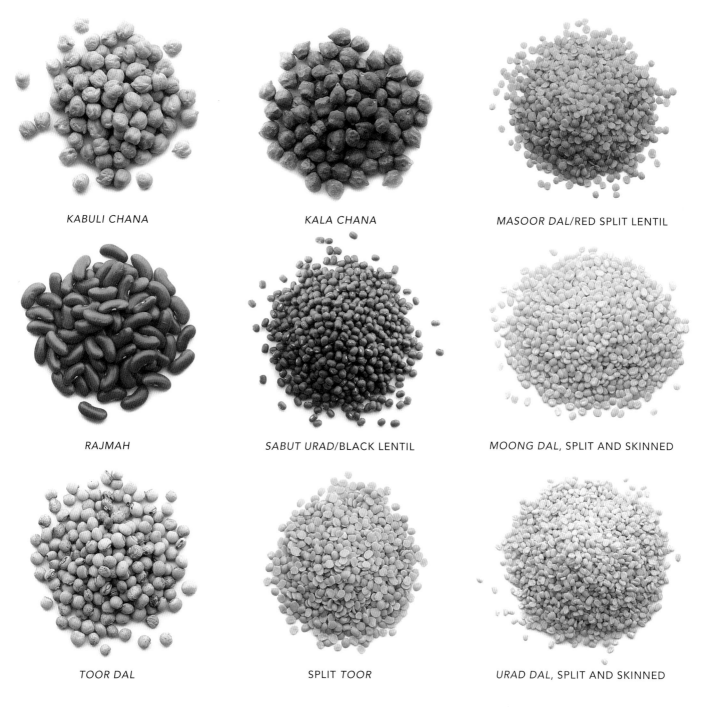

KABULI CHANA

KALA CHANA

MASOOR DAL/RED SPLIT LENTIL

RAJMAH

SABUT URAD/BLACK LENTIL

MOONG DAL, SPLIT AND SKINNED

TOOR DAL

SPLIT TOOR

URAD DAL, SPLIT AND SKINNED

Chickpeas (*chana*): Who would have thought that chickpeas could be so varied and interesting? Most of us are used to the white chickpea that is used most commonly around the world. In Hindi, it's called *kabuli chana*, and it's used in dishes that have a lot of gravy and dishes where the beans are cooked until soft, but with little gravy.

A lesser-known variety of the traditional chickpea is the black chickpea, or *kala chana*. As its name suggests, this bean looks like a chickpea, but it's about half the size and blackish brown. It's extremely high in protein and needs to be cooked longer than its white counterpart. Even after cooking, though, keep in mind that this bean is a bit tough. It will never be as soft or break down as much as other beans and lentils. But don't worry—it's still delicious. This almost meaty texture is why it's a perfect substitute for meat in kabobs and burgers.

At most Indian grocery stores, you will also see green chickpeas, or *hara chana*. These are just like black chickpeas in size and shape, but they're green in color. When cooked, the green chickpea doesn't look or taste much different from the black chickpea.

Split gram (*chana dal*): This is probably one of the most common legumes in India. It's derived from skinning and splitting the black chickpea. It makes a delicious, hearty stew. When raw, it looks a lot like the split and skinned version of *toor dal*, so be sure to label your containers.

Green *dal*, green gram (*moong, mung*): These lentils look like their black counterparts (*urad dal*) in size and shape, but they are green in color. They also cook faster than black *dal*. Also technically a bean, this legume comes in three forms: whole with the skin (*sabut moong*), split with the skin (*moong dal*), and split without the skin (yellow *moong*). This last form is one of the fastest-cooking and best-known *dals* in North India. It's easy on the stomach, so it is often made without spices to soothe a stomachache.

Kidney beans (*rajmah*): As its name suggests, this is a kidney-shaped bean that is red in color. Many types of kidney beans are available: dark red, light red, and *Jammu* or *Kashmiri rajmah*. Some prefer the *Kashmiri rajmah* because it's smaller and more delicate than the other varieties, but I prefer the light red because it breaks down better in the cooking process. Every household in North India has its own way of cooking this bean, which shows you how important it is to this region of India. Red kidney beans do contain high levels of a toxin that occurs naturally in beans and that can adversely affect you if they are eaten raw or are undercooked. Prep them by boiling in water for 10 minutes and then proceed in the Instant Pot. I have indicated this in the recipes where appropriate.

Pigeon peas: This category encompasses all of the forms of *toor dal* (*toovar*, *arhar*, and *tur*). This legume is used quite a bit in South and West India. When whole (*sabut toor*), it is small, round, and tan in color. This form is used primarily in West India. When split and skinned (*toor dal*), it has a yellowish-beige color and is the primary base for *sambhar*, a spicy soup eaten in South India with savory crepes called *dosas*. It can be purchased dry or oily. The oily version is covered with vegetable oil to increase the shelf life and to prevent contamination from insects. If you buy the oily variety, be sure to wash them thoroughly before using to get rid of that top layer of oil.

Yellow split peas: These are the dried yellow version of the green pea. They are wonderful when cooked in an Instant Pot and blended into a soup.

Indians Love Their Bread

BREAD IS JUST AS IMPORTANT AS RICE TO MANY INDIANS, ESPECIALLY IN THE northern region of Punjab, where golden wheat fields are a natural and beautiful part of the landscape. My father was raised in Bhikhi, a tiny village in the heart of this state. His father was a landowner who managed many of the wheat and mustard green fields that dominated the harvest. There, some form of bread is served with every meal, and rice is served only on special occasions.

Naan: Most non-Indians know *naan*, which has become synonymous with Indian bread. The irony here is that Indians themselves really only eat *naan* on special occasions, and we rarely make it at home. *Naan* is a leavened bread made from white flour and is traditionally cooked on the walls of a *tandoor*, or clay oven. When we eat out, my mother prefers to order *tandoori roti*, which is cooked in the same manner as *naan* but made with healthier whole-wheat flour.

Parantha: Usually eaten for breakfast, this unleavened flat bread is essentially a stuffed *roti*. You take the same dough for *rotis* and stuff a ball of it with anything from spiced potatoes to cauliflower, or even just chopped onions and chiles. *Paranthas* are usually thicker and heavier than *rotis*. Both are cooked on a heavy cast-iron griddle known as a *tava*. Toward the end of cooking, a teaspoon of oil or *ghee* is usually spread across the *parantha* to give it a golden sheen.

Puri: Talk about the ultimate comfort food. *Puris* hit the mark! The dough is a little harder than that used to make *rotis*. Once the ball of dough is rolled out thin, it is put in a deep wok-like pan, called a *karahi*, that is filled with hot oil. The flat dough will initially sink to the bottom, but as it cooks it will rise to the top of the oil in seconds and puff up.

Roti, chapati, phulka: The healthiest and most common bread in India is *roti*, unleavened flat bread that is rolled out thin by hand and heated until golden brown. Traditionally, *rotis* are made from 100 percent whole-wheat flour. Outside of India, the best way to make them is to purchase *chapati* or *aata* flour from an Indian grocery store. The type of wheat used for *chapati* flour is made from durum wheat rather than hard red. It is softer and produces fluffier *rotis* than other kinds of flour.

When buying *chapati* flour, be careful that it's not a mix of whole-wheat and white flours. The purest, made of all whole-wheat flour, will be the healthiest choice.

How to Eat Indian Food

THERE'S A LOCAL WAY TO EAT ANY CUISINE. INDIAN FOOD IS NO EXCEPTION.
In traditional North Indian households there are predominantly seven elements to any formal meal:

1. A wet curry made of veggies, legumes, or meat
2. A dry veggie dish (*sabzi*) like cauliflower and potatoes or pan-fried okra
3. Bread like *naan*, *roti*, or *puri* and/or rice
4. A side salad of sliced raw onions, cucumbers, and tomatoes with lemon juice, sea salt, black salt, and a little red chile pepper
5. *Achaar*, which is a dollop of spicy pickle made from chile peppers, lemon, or mango, or a chutney made of mint or tamarind
6. Yogurt eaten plain or savory, as *raita*, with chopped veggies and spices
7. *Papard*, a crispy, spicy blend of lentils ground wafer thin. It becomes crispy after it's heated on the stovetop

Normally, we put rice or bread on a large dinner plate along with a scoop of the dry *sabzi*. The wet curry goes in a small bowl to the side. In another bowl is the yogurt. We take a few pieces of salad and put it on our large plate along with a piece of *papard* and *achaar* or chutney.

To eat, break off a piece of the bread and make a scoop out of it. Dip one end lightly into the *achaar* or chutney, and scoop up some dry *sabzi* and then some wet curry. Once that's in your mouth, it's followed by a piece of salad—usually a piece of onion. If eating rice instead of bread, use your spoon or fork to mix the above dishes in the same order and again chase once in your mouth with some salad. Pieces of *papard* are eaten in between for crunch and spoonfuls of yogurt cool everything down. Yes, there are many tastes and textures here, but that's the point. It's like an explosion of flavors in your mouth with every bite.

These days, with the hectic schedules of parents and kids alike, it's next to impossible to sit down to such intricate meals every night. So, in my house we usually sit down with bread or rice, a dry or wet dish, salad, and yogurt. All the rest is a bonus.

2

SOUPS & LEGUMES:
LENTILS, BEANS, & PEAS

If you purchase an Instant Pot for nothing else but to make legumes, your investment will more than pay off. A pressure cooker is one of the fastest and most consistent appliances you can use to get beans, lentils, and peas, known as *dal* in Indian cuisine, on the table fast. We typically like our *dals* soupy and flavorful over rice or along with Indian bread for dipping. You can eat them alone as well, just like a soup—which is why my recipes for traditional soups and soupy legumes are combined in this chapter. While you can make legumes in an Instant Pot without soaking, to cut the cook time down a bit, I give you instructions on soaking. A technique I employ is to soak the legumes in boiled, hot water from my electric kettle for 1 hour (some legumes are soaked for less). This simple step will save you from needing to soak them overnight (though you still can) and needing to increase cook time by 15 to 20 minutes (though you still can do that as well). I provide clear instructions on various soak time in all my recipes.

Yellow Split-Pea Soup (page 51) >

RECIPES

Black Bean Soup with Tomatillo, Roasted Corn, and Jalapeño

	3 QUART	6 QUART	8 QUART
Yield	8 cups	17 cups	22 cups
Warm up	19 mins	33 mins	33 mins
Cook	20 mins	20 mins	20 mins
Cool down	10 mins NR + MR	10 mins NR + MR	10 mins NR + MR
Total time	soak + roast + 49 mins	soak + roast + 63 mins	soak + roast + 63 mins

I love that Indian and Mexican cuisines share a love of cumin seeds. This recipe came to me after weeks of trying others and not being satisfied. I wanted deeper flavor, which roasting the peppers and corn provides. I also like sneaking in healing Indian spices like turmeric whenever I can without affecting the basic taste profile of a dish.

Ingredients	3 QUART	6 QUART	8 QUART
dried black beans, picked over and washed	2 cups	4 cups	6 cups
vegetable oil	1 Tbsp	1 Tbsp	2 Tbsp
yellow or red onions, minced	1 small	1 medium	2 medium
cloves of garlic, minced	5	10	15
bay leaves	1	2	3
carrots, diced	1 medium	2 medium	3 medium
tomatillos, husk removed, diced (or celery stalks, diced)	1 (or 2)	2 (or 4)	3 (or 6)
jalapeño peppers, roasted and diced (keep seeds, membrane, and skin)	2	4	6
cumin seeds, roasted and ground	1 Tbsp	2 Tbsp	3 Tbsp
salt	1 Tbsp	2 Tbsp	3 Tbsp
ground black pepper	½ tsp	1 tsp	1½ tsp
turmeric powder	½ tsp	1 tsp	1½ tsp
Mexican hot sauce (any kind) (optional)	2 Tbsp	¼ cup	¼ cup + 2 Tbsp
water, for cooking	4 cups	8 cups	10 cups
ears of corn, roasted and kernels removed (or frozen corn, slightly thawed)	2 (or 1½ cups)	4 (or 3 cups)	6 (or 4½ cups)
lime juice	1 lime	2 limes	3 limes
chopped fresh cilantro, for garnish	¼ cup	½ cup	¾ cup

1. Soak the beans in ample boiled, hot water for at least a half hour or in room temperature water for 2 hours to overnight. Drain and discard the water.

2. Place the inner pot in your Instant Pot. Select the **SAUTE** setting and adjust to **MORE**. When the indicator flashes **HOT**, add the oil. Once the oil is hot, add the onions, garlic, and bay leaves. Stir and cook for 1 minute.

3. Add the carrots, tomatillos, and jalapeños. Stir and cook for 1 minute.

4. Press **CANCEL**. Add the black beans, cumin, salt, pepper, turmeric, hot sauce, and cooking water. Stir.

5. Lock the lid into place and make sure the pressure release valve is set to the sealing position (upwards). Press the **PRESSURE COOK** button and then press the **PRESSURE LEVEL** button until the panel reads **HIGH**. Adjust the cook time to 20 minutes.

6. Once the cooking is complete, release the pressure naturally for 10 minutes. Then manually release the remaining pressure, press **CANCEL**, and remove the lid.

7. Remove and discard the bay leaves. With a slotted spoon, take out a small amount of product (1 cup for a 3-quart IP, 2 cups for a 6-quart IP, 3 cups for an 8-quart IP) and set aside. With an immersion or regular blender, process the remaining product until smooth. *If using an immersion blender, you may need to tilt the pot so the contents don't splash.*

8. Return the removed product and add the corn, lime juice, and cilantro and stir. Serve piping hot in soup bowls or mugs and garnish with sliced avocado, crushed tortilla chips, a pinch of grated cheese, and/or a dollop of sour cream.

NOTE: I roast my peppers and corn right on my gas range. You can also roast them in the oven at 450°F for about 25 minutes, turning in between.

TRY THIS! Add some chicken or veggie sausage for an added layer of taste and texture.

Creamy Turmeric Corn Soup

Blending a bit of turmeric into this corn soup is a great way to get all the healing properties of the spice without altering the light, bright taste of the corn. Use nuts like cashews rather than dairy to make it creamy. This soup is a great start to a meal or a nourishing snack between meals.

	3 QUART	6 QUART	8 QUART
Yield	9 cups	18 cups	21 cups
Warm up	20 mins	31 mins	36 mins
Cook	5 mins	5 mins	5 mins
Cool down	5 mins NR + MR	5 mins NR + MR	5 mins NR + MR
Total time	30 mins	41 mins	46 mins

Ingredients	3 QUART	6 QUART	8 QUART
vegetable oil	1 Tbsp	2 Tbsp	3 Tbsp
turmeric powder	1 tsp	2 tsp	1 Tbsp
shallots, minced	1 small	1 medium	2 medium
potatoes (any kind), peeled and diced	1 small	1 medium	2 medium
frozen yellow corn kernels, divided	3 cups + ½ cup	6 cups + 1 cup	10 cups + 1½ cups
raw, unsalted cashews (whole or broken)	¼ cup	½ cup	1 cup
salt	1 Tbsp	2 Tbsp	3 Tbsp
ground black pepper	1 tsp	2 tsp	1 Tbsp
ground coriander	1 tsp	2 tsp	1 Tbsp
water	6 cups	12 cups	15 cups
minced fresh cilantro, for garnish	2 tsp	1 Tbsp	2 Tbsp

1. Place the inner pot in your Instant Pot. Select the **SAUTE** setting and adjust to **NORMAL**. When the indicator flashes **HOT**, add the oil. Once the oil is hot, add the turmeric, shallots, and potatoes. Stir and cook for 40 seconds until the shallots are slightly opaque.

2. Add a portion of the corn (3 cups for a 3-quart IP, 6 cups for a 6-quart IP, 10 cups for an 8-quart IP) and the cashews. Stir and cook for 1 minute. *The corn should be slightly thawed.*

3. Press **CANCEL**. Add the salt, pepper, coriander, and water. Stir.

4. Lock the lid into place and make sure the pressure release valve is set to the sealing position (upwards). Press the **PRESSURE COOK** button, and then press the **PRESSURE LEVEL** button until the panel reads **HIGH**. Adjust the cook time to 5 minutes.

5. Once the cooking is complete, release the pressure naturally for 5 minutes. Then manually release the remaining pressure. *Cover the release valve loosely with a dishcloth you don't mind staining to avoid splattering.* Press **CANCEL** and remove the lid.

6. Carefully transfer the product to a blender and process until smooth in batches. *You can use an immersion blender, but a traditional blender or Vitamix provides a smoother consistency.* Once blended, add the remaining corn, stir, and serve piping hot, garnished with the cilantro.

Toor Dal Rasam

South Indian Tomato and Tamarind Soup with Pigeon Peas

Rasam is a thin, tart, and spicy South Indian soup that is traditionally eaten with plain rice or savored after a meal on its own. I like it for breakfast as a savory and healthy start to my day. The combination of tamarind, black pepper, tomatoes, and lemon juice makes this a healing and healthy snack or meal.

	3 QUART	6 QUART	8 QUART
Yield	8 cups	15 cups	23 cups
Warm up	22 mins	35 mins	35 mins
Cook	8 mins	8 mins	8 mins
Cool down	10 mins NR + MR	10 mins NR + MR	10 mins NR + MR
Total time	40 mins + *tarka*	53 mins + *tarka*	53 mins + *tarka*

Ingredients for IP	3 QUART	6 QUART	8 QUART
whole tomatoes, cored	3 large	7 large	9 large
dhuli toor dal (dried, split, and skinned pigeon peas), picked over and washed	1 Tbsp	2 Tbsp	¼ cup
cloves of garlic, minced	3	6	8
tamarind purée	2 Tbsp	¼ cup	¼ cup + 1 Tbsp
whole black peppercorns, slightly crushed	2 tsp	1 Tbsp	1 Tbsp + 2 tsp
whole dried red chiles, broken into pieces	6	12	15
Rasam Powder (recipe on page 50)	2 Tbsp	¼ cup	¼ cup + 1 Tbsp
salt	1 Tbsp	2 Tbsp	3 Tbsp
light or dark brown sugar	1 tsp	2 tsp	1 Tbsp
red chile powder or cayenne pepper	1 tsp	2 tsp	1 Tbsp
turmeric powder	½ tsp	1 tsp	2 tsp
water	5 cups	9 cups	12 cups
lemon juice (for serving)	½ lemon	1 lemon	1 lemon
chopped fresh cilantro (for serving)	1 Tbsp	2 Tbsp	½ cup
Ingredients for *tarka*	**3 QUART**	**6 QUART**	**8 QUART**
coconut oil or *ghee*	2 Tbsp	3 Tbsp	3 Tbsp
hing (asafoetida) (optional)	2 pinches	2 pinches	2 pinches
cumin seeds	½ tsp	1 tsp	2 tsp
black mustard seeds	½ tsp	1 tsp	2 tsp
whole dried red chiles, broken into pieces	4	8	10
fresh curry leaves	10	15	20

1. Place the inner pot in your Instant Pot. Add the tomatoes, *toor dal*, garlic, tamarind, peppercorns, dried chiles, *rasam* powder, salt, sugar, red chile powder, turmeric, and water. *The tomatoes do not need to be diced. I keep the skin, but you can remove it for a smoother finish.*

2. Lock the lid into place and make sure the pressure release valve is set to the sealing position (upwards). Press the **PRESSURE COOK** button and then press the **PRESSURE LEVEL** button until the panel reads **HIGH**. Adjust the cook time to 8 minutes.

3. Once the cooking is complete, release the pressure naturally for 10 minutes. Then manually release the remaining pressure, press **CANCEL**, and remove the lid. With an immersion or regular blender, process the product until smooth. If using a regular blender, transfer the product back into the inner pot. Press the **SAUTE** button until the panel reads **LESS**. *This keeps the soup hot as you prepare the* tarka.

4. Prepare the *tarka* on the stovetop by warming the oil in a shallow pan over medium-high heat. Once the oil is hot, add the *hing*, cumin, mustard, and dried chiles and cook until the mixture sizzles, about 30 seconds. *The mustard seeds will turn greyish.* Add the curry leaves, stir, and cook for 1 minute until the leaves start to curl. *Keep a lid handy in case the oil splatters.*

5. Carefully add this mixture to the soup. Stir and let the mixture boil for 1–2 minutes to pull all the spices together. Press **CANCEL**. Add the lemon juice and cilantro. Serve piping hot as a soup or over plain basmati rice. *All the spices including the curry leaves are edible.* I love serving this soup as a starter in short glasses garnished with lemon zest for parties.

NOTE: Tamarind is key to this dish. I used paste because it's easier to find. You can also replace the paste with 1 cup of tamarind water. To make it, soak a 2-inch cube of dried tamarind pulp in 1 cup of boiling water. Strain the water, discard the pulp, and add the tamarind water to your IP.

RASAM POWDER

YIELD: **3 CUPS**

Many South Indian meals start with a small bowl of thin, spicy tomato soup called *rasam.* This is the flavorful spice blend that is used to make the delicious and nutritious soup by the same name. You can use it for soup or use it to make a quick Indian-inspired dish.

1 heaping tablespoon *chana dal* (dried, split, and skinned black chickpeas)

1 heaping tablespoon *toor dal* (dried, split, and skinned pigeon peas)

2 cups coriander seeds

½ cup cumin seeds

½ cup whole black peppercorns

½ teaspoon fenugreek seeds

10 whole dried red chiles, broken into pieces

15 fresh curry leaves, coarsely chopped

1 teaspoon turmeric powder

1. In a shallow, heavy pan, dry roast all the ingredients except the turmeric over medium heat. When putting them into the pan, start with the chickpeas and pigeon peas so they are closest to the heat and cook through. Shake or mix frequently, and watch closely that the mixture does not burn. Once the chickpeas and pigeon peas brown, the curry leaves start to curl up, and the spices smell aromatic (about 4 minutes), transfer the mixture to a large plate or bowl and allow it to cool for 15 minutes.

2. Once the mixture is cool, add the turmeric and transfer to a spice grinder or the dry jug of a powerful blender, such as a Vitamix. You may need to grind it in small batches, depending on the size of your grinder. Sift after grinding to get a finer powder. Store in an airtight container for up to 6 months.

Yellow Split-Pea Soup

with Burnt Onions and Yogurt

I describe this soup as "spring on a spoon." It's sweet, refreshing, and deceptively easy to make, especially in an Instant Pot. The taste is just a bit sweeter than its green counterpart, and the bright yellow color is a welcome change to ring in the warm months of the year.

	3 QUART	6 QUART	8 QUART
Yield	7 cups	14 cups	20 cups
Warm up	19 mins	25 mins	30 mins
Cook	15 mins	15 mins	15 mins
Cool down	10 mins NR + MR	10 mins NR + MR	10 mins NR + MRT
Total time	44 mins + *tarka*	50 mins + *tarka*	55 mins + *tarka*

Ingredients for IP	3 QUART	6 QUART	8 QUART
vegetable oil	1 Tbsp	2 Tbsp	3 Tbsp
shallots, minced	1 small	1 medium	2 medium
cloves of garlic, minced	2	4	6
dried and skinned yellow split peas, picked over and washed	2 cups	4 cups	6 cups
salt, divided	1 Tbsp + ½ tsp	2 Tbsp + 1 tsp	3 Tbsp + 2 tsp
water	6 cups	12 cups	17 cups
plain, unsweetened *hung* curd or Greek-style yogurt	1 cup	2 cups	2½ cups
roasted cumin seeds, ground (see recipe on page 23)	2 tsp	1 Tbsp	1½ Tbsp
ground black pepper	1 tsp	2 tsp	1 Tbsp
Ingredients for *tarka*	**3 QUART**	**6 QUART**	**8 QUART**
ghee or butter	1 Tbsp	2 Tbsp	3 Tbsp
yellow, red, or white onions, finely minced	1 medium	2 medium	3 medium

1. Place the inner pot in your Instant Pot. Select the **SAUTE** setting and adjust to **NORMAL**. When the indicator flashes **HOT**, add the oil. Once the oil is hot, add the shallots and garlic. Stir and cook for 1 minute until translucent.

2. Press **CANCEL**. Add the split peas, a portion of the salt (1 tablespoon for a 3-quart IP, 2 tablespoons for a 6-quart IP, 3 tablespoons for an 8-quart IP), and the water. Stir. *You can substitute green split peas for an earthier taste.*

3. Lock the lid into place. Make sure the pressure release valve is set to the sealing position (upwards). Press the **PRESSURE COOK** button and then press the **PRESSURE LEVEL** button until the panel reads **HIGH**. Adjust the cook time to 15 minutes.

4. Once the cooking is complete, release the pressure naturally for 10 minutes. Then manually release the remaining pressure, press **CANCEL**, and remove the lid. Purée the soup with an immersion or regular blender until smooth.

5. In a small bowl, whisk together the yogurt, the remaining salt, the cumin, and the black pepper.

6. On the stovetop in a shallow pan, make the onion *tarka*. Heat the *ghee* over medium-high heat, add the onions, and cook until completely burnt and crisp, about 10 minutes or longer. Stir. *Add a little more ghee if needed.*

7. To serve, place 1 cup of the soup in a bowl and top with 1 tablespoon of the spiced yogurt and 1 teaspoon of the burnt onions. *Store the unused yogurt and onion in the fridge for up to a week. When stored in the fridge, this soup gets thick and chunky. Just heat it up with a little water.*

Indian-Inspired Vegetable Soup

My mom makes the most amazing vegetable soups. This recipe is a great example of how she blends fresh vegetables with Indian lentils and spices. You may substitute any vegetables you have on hand, such as cauliflower, spinach, or broccoli. You can also try using barley or wild rice as the grain and substituting another legume for the *moong dal*.

	3 QUART	6 QUART	8 QUART
Yield	8 cups	14 cups	19 cups
Warm up	23 mins	26 mins	33 mins
Cook	4 mins	4 mins	4 mins
Cool down	5 mins NR + MR	5 mins NR + MR	5 mins NR + MR
Total time	32 mins	35 mins	42 mins

Ingredients	3 QUART	6 QUART	8 QUART
vegetable oil	1 Tbsp	2 Tbsp	3 Tbsp
hing (asafoetida) (optional)	1 pinch	2 pinches	3 pinches
cumin seeds	1 tsp	2 tsp	1 Tbsp
turmeric powder	½ tsp	1 tsp	2 tsp
cloves of garlic, minced	3	6	9
yellow or white onions, coarsely chopped	1 small	1 medium	2 medium
sabut moong dal (whole, dried green *dal* with skin), picked over and washed (not soaked)	2 Tbsp	¼ cup	⅓ cup
uncooked brown rice	2 Tbsp	¼ cup	⅓ cup
white or red quinoa	2 Tbsp	¼ cup	⅓ cup
carrots, peeled and sliced in rounds	2 medium	4 medium	5 medium
stalks celery, diced	3	6	8
diced zucchini	½ cup	1 cup	1½ cups
tomatoes, peeled and coarsely chopped	1 small	1 medium	2 medium
thinly sliced green cabbage	2 cups	4 cups	6 cups
piece of ginger, minced	1 (½-inch)	1 (1-inch)	1 (1½-inch)
whole black peppercorns, crushed	1 tsp	2 tsp	1 Tbsp
salt	2 tsp	1 Tbsp + 1 tsp	2 Tbsp
water	5 cups	10 cups	15 cups

1. Place the inner pot in your Instant Pot. Select the **SAUTE** setting and adjust to **NORMAL**. When the indicator flashes **HOT**, add the oil. Once the oil is hot, add the *hing* and cumin. Stir and cook for 1 minute until the seeds turn reddish brown. *Because the oil pools to the sides, push the spices into the oil along the border of the inner pot so they can cook fully.*

2. Add the turmeric. Stir and cook for 30 seconds.

3. Add the garlic. Stir and cook for 20 seconds.

4. Add the onions. Stir and cook for 30 seconds.

5. Add the *moong*, rice, and quinoa. Stir and cook for 20 seconds.

6. Add the carrots, celery, zucchini, and tomatoes. Stir and cook for 20 seconds.

7. Press **CANCEL**. Add the cabbage, ginger, pepper, salt, and water.

8. Lock the lid into place and make sure the pressure release valve is set to the sealing position (upwards). Press the **PRESSURE COOK** button and then press the **PRESSURE LEVEL** button until the panel reads **HIGH**. Adjust the cook time to 4 minutes.

9. Once the cooking is complete, release the pressure naturally for 5 minutes. Then manually release the remaining pressure, press **CANCEL**, and remove the lid. Serve steaming hot in bowls topped with shredded cheese (any kind) and crushed tortilla chips. *You can also blend the soup down a bit with an immersion blender before serving. Swap in other vegetables and grains to make endless variations.*

Kaali Dal

Black dal, sabut urad, whole black gram, maa, whole matpe beans

This is a staple dish in North India, where it is known as the queen of all *dals*. Usually, slow cooking is the best method to break this legume down. I was able to get the same effect by soaking the *dal* first and then pressure cooking it for a slightly longer time.

	3 QUART	6 QUART	8 QUART
Yield	9 cups	15 cups	19 cups
Warm up	19 mins	34 mins	33 mins
Cook	40 mins	40 mins	40 mins
Cool down	10 mins NR + MR	10 mins NR + MR	10 mins NR + MR
Total time	soak + 69 mins	soak + 84 mins	soak + 83 mins

Ingredients	3 QUART	6 QUART	8 QUART
sabut urad (whole, dried black *dal* with skin), picked over and washed	2 cups	4 cups	6 cups
oil or *ghee*	1 Tbsp	2 Tbsp	3 Tbsp
hing (asafoetida) (optional)	1 pinch	2 pinches	3 pinches
cumin seeds	1 tsp	2 tsp	1 Tbsp
turmeric powder	½ tsp	1 tsp	1½ tsp
yellow or red onions, puréed	1 small	1 medium	2 medium
piece of ginger, puréed	1 (1-inch)	1 (2-inch)	1 (3-inch)
cloves of garlic, puréed	2	4	6
fresh Thai or serrano chiles, stems removed and thinly sliced	1–4	2–8	3–9
tomatoes, puréed	1 medium	2 medium	3 medium
garam masala	2 tsp	1 Tbsp	2 Tbsp
ground cumin	2 tsp	1 Tbsp	2 Tbsp
ground coriander	2 tsp	1 Tbsp	2 Tbsp
red chile powder or cayenne pepper	2 tsp	1 Tbsp	2 Tbsp
salt	1 Tbsp	2 Tbsp	3 Tbsp
water, for cooking	6 cups	10 cups	13 cups
minced fresh cilantro, for garnish	2 Tbsp	¼ cup	¼ cup

1. Soak the *urad dal* in ample boiled, hot water for 1 hour or in room temperature water for 6 hours to overnight. Drain and discard the water.

2. Place the inner pot in your Instant Pot. Select the **SAUTE** setting and adjust to **MORE**. When the indicator flashes **HOT**, add the oil. Once the oil is hot, add the *hing* and cumin seeds. Stir and cook for 40 seconds until the seeds turn reddish brown. *Because the oil pools to the sides, push the spices into the oil along the border of the inner pot so they can cook fully.*

3. Add the turmeric. Stir and cook for 30 seconds.

4. Add the onions. Stir and cook for 3 minutes.

5. Add the ginger, garlic, and fresh chiles. Stir and cook for 1 minute.

6. Add the tomatoes. Stir and cook for 2 minutes.

7. Press **CANCEL**. Add the *garam masala*, ground cumin, coriander, red chile powder, salt, *urad dal*, and cooking water. Stir.

8. Lock the lid into place and make sure the pressure release valve is set to the sealing position (upwards). Press the **PRESSURE COOK** button and then press the **PRESSURE LEVEL** button until the panel reads **HIGH**. Adjust the cook time to 40 minutes.

9. Once the cooking is complete, release the pressure naturally for 10 minutes. Then manually release the remaining pressure, press **CANCEL**, and remove the lid. Garnish with the cilantro and serve with basmati rice or Indian bread like *roti* or *naan*. *All the spices are edible.*

Sabut Kaali Dal aur Rajmah

Black Dal with Kidney Beans

Whole black *dal* and kidney bean curry was a staple in my husband's childhood home. My mother-in-law makes the best I've ever tasted. It's a nice variation from the traditional black *dal* recipe. Slicing the ginger into thin strips is worth the extra effort for the heightened flavor and unique texture it provides.

	3 QUART	6 QUART	8 QUART
Yield	8 cups	16 cups	20 cups
Warm up	19 mins	34 mins	33 mins
Cook	40 mins	40 mins	40 mins
Cool down	10 mins NR + MR	10 mins NR + MR	10 mins NR + MR
Total time	soak + 69 mins	soak + 84 mins	soak + 83 mins

Ingredients	3 QUART	6 QUART	8 QUART
sabut urad (whole, dried black *dal* with skin), picked over and washed	1½ cups	3 cups	4 cups
rajmah (dried red kidney beans), picked over and washed	½ cup	1 cup	2 cups
oil or *ghee*	1 Tbsp	2 Tbsp	3 Tbsp
hing (asafoetida) (optional)	1 pinch	2 pinches	3 pinches
turmeric powder	½ tsp	1 tsp	1½ tsp
yellow or red onions, minced	1 small	1 medium	2 medium
piece of ginger, sliced into 1-inch matchsticks	1 (1-inch)	1 (2-inch)	1 (3-inch)
cloves of garlic, minced	4	8	10
fresh Thai or serrano chiles, stems removed and thinly sliced	1–4	2–8	3–9
unsalted tomato paste	1 Tbsp	2 Tbsp	3 Tbsp
garam masala	1 Tbsp	2 Tbsp	3 Tbsp
ground cumin	1 Tbsp	2 Tbsp	3 Tbsp
ground coriander	1 Tbsp	2 Tbsp	3 Tbsp
amchur (dried mango powder)	1 Tbsp	2 Tbsp	3 Tbsp
red chile powder or cayenne pepper	1 Tbsp	2 Tbsp	3 Tbsp
salt	1 Tbsp	2 Tbsp	3 Tbsp
water, for cooking	5 cups	10 cups	13 cups
chopped fresh cilantro, for garnish	2 Tbsp	¼ cup	½ cup

1. Soak the *urad dal* and *rajmah* together in ample boiled, hot water for 1 hour or in room temperature water for 6 hours to overnight. Drain and discard the water.

2. Place the inner pot in your Instant Pot. Select the **SAUTE** setting and adjust to **MORE**. When the indicator flashes **HOT**, add the oil. Once the oil is hot, add the *hing* and turmeric. Stir and cook for 40 seconds.

3. Add the onions. Stir and cook for 3 minutes.

4. Add the ginger, garlic, and fresh chiles. Stir and cook for 1 minute.

5. Press **CANCEL**. Add the tomato paste, *garam masala*, cumin, coriander, *amchur*, red chile powder, salt, *urad dal/rajmah*, and cooking water. Stir.

6. Lock the lid into place and make sure the pressure release valve is set to the sealing position (upwards). Press the **PRESSURE COOK** button and then press the **PRESSURE LEVEL** button until the panel reads **HIGH**. Adjust the cook time to 40 minutes.

7. Once the cooking is complete, release the pressure naturally for 10 minutes. Then manually release the remaining pressure, press **CANCEL**, and remove the lid. Garnish with the cilantro and serve with basmati rice or Indian bread like *roti* or *naan. All the spices are edible.*

Dal Makhani

Buttery Black *Dal*

Dal with *makhan* (butter) is a more decadent version of Indian black *dal* that has become a standard, go-to dish on Indian restaurant menus, likely because it's at once hearty and comforting. The addition of fenugreek in both the seed and the herb forms adds a gourmet quality to this homestyle dish.

	3 QUART	6 QUART	8 QUART
Yield	8 cups	16 cups	20 cups
Warm up	18 mins	34 mins	33 mins
Cook	40 mins	40 mins	40 mins
Cool down	10 mins NR + MR	10 mins NR + MR	10 mins NR + MR
Total time	soak + 68 mins	soak + 84 mins	soak + 83 mins

Ingredients	3 QUART	6 QUART	8 QUART
sabut urad (whole, dried black *dal* with skin), picked over and washed	1½ cups	3 cups	4 cups
rajmah (dried red kidney beans), picked over and washed	½ cup	1 cup	2 cups
ghee or vegetable oil	1 Tbsp	2 Tbsp	3 Tbsp
hing (asafoetida) (optional)	1 pinch	2 pinches	3 pinches
cumin seeds	2 tsp	1 Tbsp + 1 tsp	1 Tbsp + 2 tsp
turmeric powder	½ tsp	1 tsp	1½ tsp
cinnamon stick	1 (1-inch)	1 (2-inch)	1 (3-inch)
cassia leaves (or bay leaves)	1 (or 2)	1 (or 3)	2 (or 4)
fenugreek seeds	½ tsp	1 tsp	2 tsp
yellow or red onions, puréed	1 small	1 medium	2 medium
piece of ginger, puréed	1 (1-inch)	1 (2-inch)	1 (3-inch)
cloves of garlic, puréed	3	6	8
fresh Thai or serrano chiles, stems removed and thinly sliced	1–4	2–8	3–9
unsalted tomato paste	¼ cup	½ cup	¾ cup
garam masala	2 tsp	1 Tbsp + 1 tsp	2 Tbsp
ground cumin	2 tsp	1 Tbsp + 1 tsp	2 Tbsp
ground coriander	2 tsp	1 Tbsp + 1 tsp	2 Tbsp
red chile powder or cayenne pepper	2 tsp	1 Tbsp + 1 tsp	2 Tbsp
cardamom seeds, ground (optional)	1 tsp	1 Tbsp + 1 tsp	1 Tbsp + 2 tsp
kasoori methi (dried fenugreek leaves), lightly hand crushed to release flavor	2 Tbsp	¼ cup	¾ cup
salt	1 Tbsp	2 Tbsp	3 Tbsp
water, for cooking	5 cups	10 cups	13 cups
cream (dairy or alternative like cashew)	¼ cup	½ cup	¾ cup

1. Soak the *urad dal* and *rajmah* together in ample boiled, hot water for at least 1 hour or in room temperature water for 6 hours to overnight. Drain and discard the water.

2. Place the inner pot in your Instant Pot. Select the **SAUTE** setting and adjust to **MORE**. When the indicator flashes **HOT**, add the *ghee*. Once the *ghee* is hot, add the *hing*, cumin seeds, turmeric, cinnamon, and cassia or bay leaves. Stir and cook for 1 minute until the seeds turn reddish brown. *Because the oil pools to the sides, push the spices into the oil along the border of the inner pot so they can cook fully.*

3. Add the fenugreek seeds. Stir and cook for 30 seconds. *Be careful not to overcook, as these seeds get bitter quickly.*

4. Add the onions. Stir and cook for 3 minutes.

5. Add the ginger, garlic, and fresh chiles. Stir and cook for 1 minute.

6. Press **CANCEL**. Add the tomato paste, *garam masala*, ground cumin, coriander, red chile powder, cardamom, *kasoori methi*, salt, *urad dal/rajmah*, and cooking water. Stir.

7. Lock the lid into place and make sure the pressure release valve is set to the sealing position (upwards). Press the **PRESSURE COOK** button and then press the **PRESSURE LEVEL** button until the panel reads **HIGH**. Adjust the cook time to 40 minutes.

8. Once the cooking is complete, release the pressure naturally for 10 minutes. Then manually release the remaining pressure, press **CANCEL**, and remove the lid. Remove and discard the cinnamon stick and cassia or bay leaves or leave them in for flavor and eat around them. *All the other spices are edible.* Gently fold in the cream and stir. Serve with basmati rice or Indian bread like *roti* or *naan*.

Black *Dal* with Kidney Beans and Chickpeas

	3 QUART	6 QUART	8 QUART
Yield	7 cups	15 cups	20 cups
Warm up	19 mins	34 mins	35 mins
Cook	40 mins	40 mins	40 mins
Cool down	10 mins NR + MR	10 mins NR + MR	10 mins NR + MR
Total time	soak + roast + 69 mins	soak + roast + 84 mins	soak + roast + 85 mins

I was first introduced to this recipe in Raghavan Iyer's *660 Curries* and have modified it for the Instant Pot. This dish is a meal in itself. I refer to it as "Indian Super Bowl Chili" because we like to make a big batch of it on game day and turn it into a zesty dip with some cheese and crackers.

Ingredients	3 QUART	6 QUART	8 QUART
sabut urad (whole, dried black *dal* with skin), picked over and washed	¾ cup	1½ cups	2 cups
kabuli chana (dried white chickpeas), picked over and washed	¾ cup	1½ cups	2 cups
rajmah (dried red kidney beans), picked over and washed	¾ cup	1½ cups	2 cups
yellow or red onions, coarsely chopped	1 small	1 medium	2 medium
piece of ginger, coarsely chopped	1 (1-inch)	1 (2-inch)	1 (3-inch)
cloves of garlic	2	4	6
fresh Thai or serrano chiles, stems removed, coarsely chopped	1–3	2–6	3–7
cumin seeds	2 tsp	1 Tbsp + 1 tsp	2 Tbsp
coriander seeds	2 tsp	1 Tbsp + 1 tsp	2 Tbsp
oil or *ghee*	1 Tbsp	2 Tbsp	3 Tbsp
hing (asafoetida) (optional)	1 pinch	2 pinches	3 pinches
turmeric powder	½ tsp	1 tsp	1½ tsp
cassia leaves (or bay leaves)	1 (or 1)	1 (or 2)	2 (or 3)
green cardamom pods, lightly crushed (keep the husks)	1	2	3
cinnamon sticks	1 (2-inch)	2 (2-inch)	3 (2-inch)
red chile powder or cayenne pepper	2 tsp	1 Tbsp + 1 tsp	2 Tbsp
unsalted tomato paste	2 Tbsp	¼ cup	½ cup
salt	1 Tbsp	2 Tbsp	3 Tbsp
water, for cooking	5 cups	10 cups	13 cups
chopped fresh cilantro, for garnish	1 Tbsp	2 Tbsp	3 Tbsp

1. Soak the *urad dal*, *chana*, and *rajmah* together in ample boiled, hot water for at least 1 hour or in room temperature water for 6 hours to overnight. Drain and discard the water.

2. In a food processor, grind the onions, ginger, garlic, and fresh chiles together until smooth. *The mixture will be slightly watery from the onion.* Set aside.

3. On the stovetop, place the cumin and coriander seeds in a dry, shallow pan and heat over medium-high. Roast for 2 to 4 minutes until the seeds turn reddish brown. Shake the pan a few times or stir. Be careful not to overcook or they will burn. Transfer the seeds to a dish to cool for at least 5 minutes and then grind them into a powder using a mortar and pestle or a coffee grinder reserved for spices. Set aside.

4. Place the inner pot in your Instant Pot. Select the **SAUTE** setting and adjust to **MORE**. When the indicator flashes **HOT**, add the oil. Once the oil is hot, add the *hing*, turmeric, cassia or bay leaves, cardamom, and cinnamon. Stir and cook for 1 minute.

5. Add the onion mixture from Step 2. Stir and cook for 3 minutes.

6. Press **CANCEL**. Add the cumin-coriander blend from Step 3, red chile powder, tomato paste, salt, *urad/chana/rajmah*, and cooking water. Stir.

7. Lock the lid into place and make sure the pressure release valve is set to the sealing position (upwards). Press the **PRESSURE COOK** button and then press the **PRESSURE LEVEL** button until the panel reads **HIGH**. Adjust the cook time to 40 minutes.

8. Once the cooking is complete, release the pressure naturally for 10 minutes. Then manually release the remaining pressure, press **CANCEL**, and remove the lid. Remove and discard the cassia or bay leaves and cinnamon. *All the other spices are edible.* Garnish with the cilantro and serve as a hearty stew.

Urad Dal Chilkha

Split Black *Dal*

This is one of my favorite *dals* because it's so easy to make and comes out incredibly rich and creamy. The creaminess comes from the way this *dal* breaks down after cooking rather than actual cream. Using legumes with the skin intact makes this dish more nutritious. Don't overcook this one, as it tends to get a little bitter.

	3 QUART	6 QUART	8 QUART
Yield	8 cups	16 cups	20 cups
Warm up	18 mins	26 mins	29 mins
Cook	15 mins	15 mins	15 mins
Cool down	10 mins NR + MR	10 mins NR + MR	10 mins NR + MR
Total time	soak + 43 mins	soak + 51 mins	soak + 54 mins

Ingredients	3 QUART	6 QUART	8 QUART
urad dal chilkha (split, dried black *dal* with skin), picked over and washed	2 cups	4 cups	6 cups
oil or *ghee*	1 Tbsp	2 Tbsp	3 Tbsp
hing (asafoetida) (optional)	1 pinch	2 pinches	3 pinches
cumin seeds	2 tsp	1 Tbsp + 1 tsp	2 Tbsp
turmeric powder	½ tsp	1 tsp	1½ tsp
yellow or red onions, minced	1 small	1 medium	2 medium
piece of ginger, puréed	1 (1-inch)	1 (2-inch)	1 (3-inch)
cloves of garlic, puréed	3	6	8
fresh Thai or serrano chiles, stems removed and thinly sliced	1–4	2–8	3–9
tomatoes, puréed	1 medium	2 medium	3 medium
unsalted tomato paste	1 Tbsp	2 Tbsp	3 Tbsp
garam masala	2 tsp	1 Tbsp + 1 tsp	2 Tbsp
red chile powder or cayenne pepper	2 tsp	1 Tbsp + 1 tsp	2 Tbsp
salt	1 Tbsp	2 Tbsp	3 Tbsp
water, for cooking	6 cups	9 cups	13 cups

1. Soak the *urad dal* in ample boiled, hot water for 10 minutes or in room temperature water for 1 hour to overnight. Drain and discard the water.

2. Place the inner pot in your Instant Pot. Select the **SAUTE** setting and adjust to **MORE**. When the indicator flashes **HOT**, add the oil. Once the oil is hot, add the *hing* and cumin. Stir and cook for 40 seconds until the seeds turn reddish brown. *Because the oil pools to the sides, push the spices into the oil along the border of the inner pot so they can cook fully.*

3. Add the turmeric. Stir and cook for 30 seconds.

4. Add the onions. Stir and cook for 3 minutes.

5. Add the ginger, garlic, and fresh chiles. Stir and cook for 2 minutes.

6. Press **CANCEL**. Add the tomatoes, tomato paste, *garam masala*, red chile powder, salt, *urad dal*, and cooking water. Stir.

7. Lock the lid into place and make sure the pressure release valve is set to the sealing position (upwards). Press the **PRESSURE COOK** button and then press the **PRESSURE LEVEL** button until the panel reads **HIGH**. Adjust the cook time to 15 minutes.

8. Once the cooking is complete, release the pressure naturally for 10 minutes. Then manually release the remaining pressure, press **CANCEL**, and remove the lid. Serve with basmati rice or Indian bread like *roti* or *naan*. *All the spices are edible.*

TRY THIS! Substitute split green *moong dal* with skin for the split black *dal* for a slightly different taste.

Dhuli Moong Dal

Simplest of Simple Yellow *Dal*

Split *moong dal* is a staple in Punjabi households (it looks yellow) and should be very thin and soupy. Some of my testers questioned my legume to water ratio. It is not a typo. When this *dal* hits the rice you simply slurp up all the flavors. Did I say slurp? Yes, I did!

	3 QUART	6 QUART	8 QUART
Yield	7 cups	14 cups	20 cups
Warm up	20 mins	29 mins	26 mins
Cook	3 mins	3 mins	3 mins
Cool down	10 mins NR + MR	10 mins NR + MR	10 mins NR + MR
Total time	33 mins	42 mins	39 mins

Ingredients	3 QUART	6 QUART	8 QUART
oil or *ghee*	1 Tbsp	2 Tbsp	3 Tbsp
hing (asafoetida) (optional)	1 pinch	2 pinches	3 pinches
cumin seeds	1 tsp	2 tsp	1 Tbsp
turmeric powder	½ tsp	1 tsp	2 tsp
yellow or red onions, minced	½ small	1 medium	1½ medium
piece of ginger, minced	1 (1-inch)	1 (2-inch)	1 (3-inch)
cloves of garlic, minced	2	4	6
fresh Thai or serrano chiles, stems removed and thinly sliced	½–3	1–6	2–8
garam masala	2 tsp	1 Tbsp	1 Tbsp + 2 tsp
ground coriander	1 tsp	2 tsp	1 Tbsp
red chile powder or cayenne pepper	1 tsp	2 tsp	1 Tbsp
salt	1 Tbsp	2 Tbsp	3 Tbsp
dhuli moong dal (dried, split, and skinned yellow *moong*), picked over and washed (not soaked)	1 cup	2 cups	3 cups
water	6 cups	12 cups	18 cups
chopped fresh cilantro, for garnish	1 Tbsp	2 Tbsp	3 Tbsp
minced onion, for garnish	1 Tbsp	2 Tbsp	3 Tbsp
minced fresh green chiles, for garnish	1 Tbsp	2 Tbsp	3 Tbsp

1. Place the inner pot in your Instant Pot. Select the **SAUTE** setting and adjust to **MORE**. When the indicator flashes **HOT**, add the oil. Once the oil is hot, add the *hing* and cumin. Stir and cook for 40 seconds until the seeds turn reddish brown. *Because the oil pools to the sides, push the spices into the oil along the border of the pot so they can cook fully.*

2. Add the turmeric. Stir and cook for 30 seconds.

3. Add the onions. Stir and cook for 1 minute.

4. Add the ginger, garlic, and fresh chiles. Stir and cook for 1 minute.

5. Press **CANCEL**. Add the *garam masala*, coriander, red chile powder, salt, *moong dal*, and water. Stir.

6. Lock the lid into place. Make sure the pressure release valve is set to the sealing position (upwards). Press the **PRESSURE COOK** button and then press the **PRESSURE LEVEL** button until the panel reads **HIGH**. Adjust the cook time to 3 minutes.

7. Once the cooking is complete, release the pressure naturally for 10 minutes. Then manually release the remaining pressure, press **CANCEL**, and remove the lid. *Cover the release valve loosely with a dishcloth you don't mind staining to avoid splattering.* Add the cilantro, onion, and fresh chiles and serve over basmati rice or enjoy as a soup. *All the spices are edible.*

TRY THIS! Chop up about 2 cups of fresh Swiss chard and add it at the very end. Cover with the lid slightly ajar so the greens wilt before serving.

Gujarati *Toor Dal*

Gujarati Pigeon Pea *Dal*

The sweet and sour component of this dish reflects the importance of sweet notes in food from the Indian state of Gujarat, while the peanuts add a distinctive crunch. Though I am Punjabi and love my fiery curries, I have to say I am addicted to this dish, especially served over plain rice with a touch of *ghee*. It is utterly delicious!

Ingredients for IP	3 QUART	6 QUART	8 QUART
dhuli toor dal (dried, split, and skinned pigeon peas), picked over and washed	1½ cups	3 cups	4½ cups
raw, unsalted peanuts (with or without skin)	2 Tbsp	¼ cup	½ cup
tamarind purée	1 Tbsp	2 Tbsp	3 Tbsp
water, for cooking	6 cups	8 cups	15 cups
gur (jaggery) or light brown sugar	1 Tbsp	2 Tbsp	3 Tbsp
salt	1 Tbsp	2 Tbsp	3 Tbsp

Ingredients for *tarka*	3 QUART	6 QUART	8 QUART
oil or *ghee*	2 Tbsp	3 Tbsp	3 Tbsp
hing (asafoetida) (optional)	1 pinch	2 pinches	3 pinches
turmeric powder	½ tsp	1 tsp	2 tsp
fresh curry leaves	10	15	20
cassia leaf (or bay leaves)	1 (or 2)	1 (or 3)	1 (or 3)
whole cloves	2	4	6
cinnamon stick	1 (1-inch)	1 (2-inch)	1 (3-inch)
whole dried red chiles, broken into pieces	4	8	12
black mustard seeds	½ tsp	1 tsp	1 tsp
cumin seeds	½ tsp	1 tsp	1½ tsp
fenugreek seeds	½ tsp	1 tsp	1 tsp
piece of ginger, minced	1 (1-inch)	1 (2-inch)	1 (3-inch)
fresh Thai or serrano chiles, stems removed and sliced lengthwise	1–3	2–6	4–12
tomatoes, diced	1 small	1 medium	2 medium
lemon juice	1 lemon	1½ lemons	2 lemons
chopped fresh cilantro, for garnish	2 Tbsp	3 Tbsp	¼ cup

	3 QUART	6 QUART	8 QUART
Yield	7½ cups	14 cups	22 cups
Warm up	22 mins	33 mins	35 mins
Cook	8 mins	8 mins	8 mins
Cool down	10 mins NR + MR	10 mins NR + MR	10 mins NR + MR
Total time	soak + 40 mins + *tarka* + sauté	soak + 51 mins + *tarka* + sauté	soak + 53 mins + *tarka* + sauté

1. Soak the *toor dal* in ample boiled, hot water for at least 10 minutes or in room temperature water for at least 20 minutes. Drain and discard the water.

2. In a separate bowl, soak the peanuts in room temperature water for at least 20 minutes. Set aside.

3. Place the inner pot in your Instant Pot and add the *toor dal*, tamarind, and cooking water. Lock the lid into place and make sure the pressure release valve is set to the sealing position (upwards). Press the **PRESSURE COOK** button and then press the **PRESSURE LEVEL** button until the panel reads **HIGH**. Adjust the cook time to 8 minutes.

4. Once the cooking is complete, release the pressure naturally for 10 minutes. Then manually release the remaining pressure, press **CANCEL**, and remove the lid. *Cover the release valve with a dishcloth you don't mind staining to avoid splattering. Use the condensation collector cup to catch any liquid that comes out of the back—just dump it back into the pot once all the pressure has released.*

5. With a regular or immersion blender, process the cooked *dal* until it is completely smooth. *If using an immersion blender, you may need to tilt the pot so the contents don't splash. If using a regular blender, return the product to the Instant Pot once blended.*

6. Add the drained peanuts, sugar, and salt. Stir and set aside.

7. Prepare the *tarka* on the stovetop by warming the oil in a shallow pan over medium-high heat. Once the oil is hot, add the *hing*, turmeric, curry leaves, cassia or bay leaves, cloves, cinnamon, dried chiles, mustard, cumin, and fenugreek. Stir and cook for 1 minute until the seeds sizzle. *Don't overcook because the fenugreek can become bitter, but be sure the curry leaves cook through and turn slightly brown. Keep a lid handy—the oil can splatter.*

8. Add the ginger, fresh chiles, and tomatoes. Stir well and cook for 1–2 minutes.

9. Carefully transfer this mixture to the cooked *dal* and stir.

10. Press the **SAUTE** button, adjust to **NORMAL**, and simmer for 3–4 minutes. *This helps pull the dal and tarka together. If the contents splatter, just place a lid slightly ajar over the pot.*

11. Press **CANCEL**. Add the lemon juice and cilantro. Stir again and serve piping hot over plain basmati rice. *You can remove the bay leaves, cloves, and cinnamon stick or leave them in for flavor and eat around them—all the other spices are edible, including the curry leaves.*

Palak aur Dhuli Moong Dal

Simple Spinach and *Dal* Soup

Yellow *moong dal* and spinach are perfect together. Both require minimal cooking and once finished will make a dish that you'll find oddly addictive. It's not only delicious over rice, but perfect as a simple bowl of soup on its own. This is one of the few recipes I prefer without any added onions or fresh chiles.

	3 QUART	6 QUART	8 QUART
Yield	7 cups	14 cups	20 cups
Warm up	19 mins	29 mins	25 mins
Cook	3 mins	3 mins	3 mins
Cool down	10 mins NR + MR	10 mins NR + MR	10 mins NR + MR
Total time	32 mins	42 mins	38 mins

Ingredients	3 QUART	6 QUART	8 QUART
oil or *ghee*	1 Tbsp	2 Tbsp	3 Tbsp
turmeric powder	½ tsp	1 tsp	1½ tsp
cumin seeds	½ tsp	1 tsp	2 tsp
cassia leaf (or bay leaves)	1 (or 1)	1 (or 2)	2 (or 3)
piece of ginger, minced	1 (1-inch)	1 (2-inch)	1 (3-inch)
cloves of garlic, minced	2	4	6
garam masala	½ tsp	1 tsp	1½ tsp
ground coriander	½ tsp	1 tsp	1½ tsp
unsalted tomato paste	1 Tbsp	2 Tbsp	3 Tbsp
salt	1 Tbsp	2 Tbsp	3 Tbsp
firmly packed spinach leaves, coarsely chopped	3 cups	6 cups	8 cups
dhuli moong dal (dried, split, and skinned yellow *moong*), picked over and washed (not soaked)	1 cup	2 cups	3 cups
water	6 cups	12 cups	18 cups

1. Place the inner pot in your Instant Pot. Select the **SAUTE** setting and adjust to **MORE**. When the indicator flashes **HOT**, add the oil. Once the oil is hot, add the turmeric, cumin, and cassia or bay leaves. Stir and cook for 40 seconds until the seeds turn reddish brown. *Because the oil pools to the sides, push the spices into the oil along the border of the pot so they can cook fully.*

2. Add the ginger and garlic. Stir and cook for 40 seconds.

3. Press **CANCEL**. Add the *garam masala*, coriander, tomato paste, salt, spinach, *moong dal*, and water. Stir.

4. Lock the lid into place. Make sure that the pressure release valve is set to the sealing position (upwards). Press the **PRESSURE COOK** button and then press the **PRESSURE LEVEL** button until the panel reads **HIGH**. Adjust the cook time to 3 minutes.

5. Once the cooking is complete, release the pressure naturally for 10 minutes. Then manually release the remaining pressure, press **CANCEL**, and remove the lid. *Cover the release valve loosely with a dishcloth you don't mind staining to avoid splattering.* Remove and discard the cassia or bay leaves and serve over basmati rice or eat as a soup. *All the other spices are edible.*

Palak aur Sabut Moong Dal

Spinach and Whole *Moong Dal*

My Nisha *mamiji* (aunt) in Chandigarh, India, gave me the recipe for this *dal*. Talk about packed with nutrition! It mixes the whole green *moong* with iron-rich spinach to create a dish you'll love making again and again. While the split and skinned version only takes minutes to cook in the Instant Pot, this whole version with the skin does take longer.

	3 QUART	6 QUART	8 QUART
Yield	8 cups	16 cups	20 cups
Warm up	18 mins	31 mins	33 mins
Cook	25 mins	25 mins	25 mins
Cool down	10 mins NR + MR	10 mins NR + MR	10 mins NR + MR
Total time	soak + 53 mins	soak + 66 mins	soak + 68 mins

Ingredients	3 QUART	6 QUART	8 QUART
sabut moong dal (whole, dried green *dal* with skin), picked over and washed	2 cups	4 cups	6 cups
oil or *ghee*	1 Tbsp	2 Tbsp	3 Tbsp
hing (asafoetida) (optional)	1 pinch	2 pinches	3 pinches
cumin seeds	2 tsp	1 Tbsp	1 Tbsp + 2 tsp
turmeric powder	½ tsp	1 tsp	2 tsp
yellow or red onions, minced	1 small	1 medium	2 medium
piece of ginger, minced	1 (1-inch)	1 (2-inch)	1 (3-inch)
cloves of garlic, minced	3	6	8
fresh Thai or serrano chiles, stems removed and thinly sliced	1–4	2–8	3–10
tomatoes, diced or puréed	1 small	1 medium	2 medium
garam masala	2 tsp	1 Tbsp	2 Tbsp
ground coriander	2 tsp	1 Tbsp	2 Tbsp
red chile powder or cayenne pepper	2 tsp	1 Tbsp	2 Tbsp
salt	1 Tbsp	2 Tbsp	3 Tbsp
water, for cooking	6 cups	10 cups	11 cups
firmly packed spinach leaves, chopped	2 cups	4 cups	6 cups

1. Soak the *moong dal* in ample boiled, hot water for 10 minutes or in room temperature water for 20 minutes. Drain and discard the water.

2. Place the inner pot in your Instant Pot. Select the **SAUTE** setting and adjust to **MORE**. When the indicator flashes **HOT**, add the oil. Once the oil is hot, add the *hing* and cumin. Stir and cook for 40 seconds until the seeds turn reddish brown. *Because the oil pools to the sides, push the spices into the oil so they fully cook.*

3. Add the turmeric. Stir and cook for 30 seconds.

4. Add the onions. Stir and cook for 2 minutes.

5. Add the ginger, garlic, and fresh chiles. Stir and cook for 1 minute.

6. Press **CANCEL**. Add the tomatoes, *garam masala*, coriander, red chile powder, salt, *moong dal*, and cooking water. Stir.

7. Lock the lid into place and make sure the pressure release valve is set to the sealing position (upwards). Press the **PRESSURE COOK** button and then press the **PRESSURE LEVEL** button until the panel reads **HIGH**. Adjust the cook time to 25 minutes.

8. Once the cooking is complete, release the pressure naturally for 10 minutes. Then manually release the remaining pressure, press **CANCEL**, and remove the lid. *Cover the release valve loosely with a dishcloth you don't mind staining to avoid splattering.* Add the spinach, stir, and place the lid slightly ajar on the pot for a minute or two so the steam wilts the spinach. Serve with basmati rice or Indian bread like *roti* or *naan. All the spices are edible.*

TRY THIS! Make this dish with other greens including kale, mustard, or pea shoots, or make it without the spinach—the more traditional way to eat it.

Khata Sabut Toor Dal

Tart Whole Pigeon Peas

My experimentation with whole *toor dal* paid off with a fast, easy recipe that produces a wonderful, almost meaty accompaniment to any meal as a side salad. Feel free to swap out the *toor dal* for any whole legume, including chickpeas, kidney beans, or black beans.

	3 QUART	6 QUART	8 QUART
Yield	5 cups	10 cups	16 cups
Warm up	11 mins	15 mins	17 mins
Cook	35 mins	35 mins	35 mins
Cool down	10 mins NR + MR	10 mins NR + MR	10 mins NR + MR
Total time	soak + 56 mins + tarka	soak + 60 mins + tarka	soak + 62 mins + tarka

Ingredients for IP	3 QUART	6 QUART	8 QUART
sabut toor dal (whole, dried pigeon peas with skin), picked over and washed	2 cups	4 cups	6 cups
water, for cooking	1 cup	2 cups	3 cups

Ingredients for *tarka*	3 QUART	6 QUART	8 QUART
vegetable oil	1 Tbsp	2 Tbsp	3 Tbsp
black mustard seeds	1 tsp	1½ tsp	2 tsp
fresh curry leaves	10–12	12–15	15–20
yellow or red onions, minced	1 small	1 medium	2 medium
piece of ginger, puréed	1 (1-inch)	1 (2-inch)	1 (3-inch)
cloves of garlic, puréed	2	4	6
fresh Thai or serrano chiles, stems removed and thinly sliced	1–4	2–8	3–9
whole dried red chiles, slightly crushed	5–6	10–12	12–15
ground coriander	2 tsp	1 Tbsp	1 Tbsp + 2 tsp
salt	1 Tbsp	2 Tbsp	3 Tbsp
lemon juice	1 lemon	2 lemons	2½ lemons

1. Soak the *toor dal* in ample boiled, hot water for 1 hour or in room temperature water for at least 6 hours to overnight. Drain and discard the water.

2. Place the inner pot in your Instant Pot. Add the *dal* and cooking water. Lock the lid into place and make sure the pressure release valve is set to the sealing position (upwards). Press the **PRESSURE COOK** button and then press the **PRESSURE LEVEL** button until the panel reads **HIGH**. Adjust the cook time to 35 minutes.

3. Once the cooking is complete, release the pressure naturally for 10 minutes. Then manually release the remaining pressure, press **CANCEL**, and remove the lid. *If there is too much water, drain it off or simply transfer the* dal *to a bowl with a slotted spoon. This should be a dry dish.*

4. Make the *tarka* on the stovetop by heating the oil in a shallow pan over medium-high heat. Once the oil is hot, add the mustard seeds and cook until they turn greyish. *You may need a lid to keep the oil from splattering.* Carefully add the curry leaves, onions, ginger, garlic, fresh chiles, dried chiles, and coriander. Stir and cook until the onions brown, about 2 minutes.

5. Add this mixture to the cooked *dal* along with the salt and lemon juice. Stir and enjoy with *roti* or *naan*, or as a side salad. *All the spices are edible.*

Parippu Curry

South Indian Lentils with Curry Leaves

In North India, legumes and lentils are called *dals*, while in South India they are called *parippu*. This recipe uses red split masoor lentils and holds to tradition by including curry leaves and coconut milk. I've adapted it for the Instant Pot beautifully. The key was to avoid overcooking this fast-cooking lentil in the pressure cooker.

	3 QUART	6 QUART	8 QUART
Yield	8 cups	15 cups	19 cups
Warm up	19 mins	29 mins	31 mins
Cook	7 mins	7 mins	7 mins
Cool down	MR	MR	MR
Total time	26 mins	36 mins	38 mins

Ingredients	3 QUART	6 QUART	8 QUART
coconut oil	1 Tbsp	2 Tbsp	2 Tbsp
turmeric powder	½ tsp	1 tsp	1½ tsp
cumin seeds	1 tsp	2 tsp	1 Tbsp
black mustard seeds	½ tsp	1 tsp	1½ tsp
fresh curry leaves	5–8	8–12	12–18
yellow or red onions, minced	1 small	1 medium	2 medium
fresh Thai or serrano chiles, stems removed and thinly sliced	1–4	2–8	3–9
tomatoes, diced	1 medium	2 medium	3 medium
ground cumin	2 tsp	1 Tbsp + 1 tsp	2 Tbsp
ground coriander	2 tsp	1 Tbsp + 1 tsp	2 Tbsp
salt	1 Tbsp	2 Tbsp	3 Tbsp
dhuli masoor dal (dried, split, and skinned red lentils), picked over and washed (not soaked)	2 cups	4 cups	6 cups
water	4 cups	8 cups	10 cups
regular or light coconut milk, divided	¾ cup + ¼ cup	1½ cups + ½ cup	2 cups + 1 cup

1. Place the inner pot in your Instant Pot. Select the **SAUTE** setting and adjust to **MORE**. When the indicator flashes **HOT**, add the oil. Once the oil is hot, add the turmeric and cumin seeds and cook for 40 seconds until the seeds turn reddish brown. *Because the oil pools to the sides, push the seeds into the oil along the border of the inner pot so they can cook fully.*

2. Add the mustard seeds and curry leaves. *Keep a lid handy, as the moisture in the curry leaves can cause the oil to splatter.* Stir and cook for 1 minute until the seeds turn greyish and the leaves curl up.

3. Add the onions. Stir and cook for 2 minutes.

4. Add the fresh chiles. Stir and cook for 1 minute.

5. Add the tomatoes. Stir and cook for 1 minute.

6. Press **CANCEL**. Add the ground cumin, coriander, salt, *masoor dal*, water, and a portion of the coconut milk (¾ cup for a 3-quart IP, 1½ cups for a 6-quart IP, 2 cups for an 8-quart IP). Stir. *Uncooked split and skinned* masoor dal *starts reddish and turns yellow after cooking.*

7. Lock the lid into place and make sure the pressure release valve is set to the sealing position (upwards). Press the **PRESSURE COOK** button and then press the **PRESSURE LEVEL** button until the panel reads **HIGH**. Adjust the cook time to 7 minutes.

8. Once the cooking is complete, release the pressure manually, press **CANCEL**, and remove the lid. Gently fold in the remaining coconut milk and stir. *All the spices are edible, including the curry leaves.* Enjoy over plain rice with a dollop of *ghee* or as a soup.

Sambhar (pictured right; see recipe on page 70) is one of the most popular South Indian stews. Traditionally, it is eaten for breakfast or lunch with steamed *idlis* or large paper-thin savory crepes called *dosas*. My friends and family are still amazed that it can taste so authentic coming from an Instant Pot.

Sambhar

South Indian Pigeon Peas and Vegetable Stew

This is a perfect dish in the winter when there are root vegetables at the market like parsnips and turnips. You can make this with store-bought *sambhar* powder, but I guarantee if you make the mix yourself you will appreciate the robust flavor.

	3 QUART	6 QUART	8 QUART
Yield	8 cups	16 cups	22 cups
Warm up	19 mins	34 mins	31 mins
Cook	8 mins	8 mins	8 mins
Cool down	10 mins NR + MR	10 mins NR + MR	10 mins NR + MR
Total time	37 mins + tarka	52 mins + tarka	49 mins + tarka

Ingredients for IP	3 QUART	6 QUART	8 QUART
vegetable oil	1 Tbsp	2 Tbsp	3 Tbsp
hing (asafoetida) (optional)	1 pinch	2 pinches	3 pinches
turmeric powder	½ tsp	1 tsp	1½ tsp
whole dried red chiles, broken into pieces	2	4	12
yellow onions, coarsely chopped	1 small	1 medium	2 medium
fresh Thai or serrano chiles, stems removed and sliced lengthwise	1–4	2–8	3–10
tomatoes, coarsely chopped	1 small	1 medium	2 medium
carrots, sliced in ½-inch rounds	1 medium	2 medium	3 medium
daikon, sliced in 2-inch matchsticks	1 medium	2 medium	3 medium
turnips, diced	1 small	1 medium	2 medium
russet, Yukon Gold, or red potatoes, peeled and cut into 1½-inch chunks	1 small	1 medium	2 medium
dhuli toor dal (dried, split, and skinned pigeon peas), picked over and washed (not soaked)	1 cup	2 cups	3 cups
sambhar powder (see recipe on page 71)	2 Tbsp	¼ cup	¼ cup + 2 Tbsp
red chile powder or cayenne pepper	1 tsp	2 tsp	1 Tbsp
salt	1 Tbsp	2 Tbsp	3 Tbsp
tamarind purée	1 Tbsp	2 Tbsp	3 Tbsp
water	5 cups	10 cups	14 cups

Ingredients for *tarka*	3 QUART	6 QUART	8 QUART
vegetable oil	2 Tbsp	2 Tbsp	2 Tbsp
black mustard seeds	½ tsp	1 tsp	1½ tsp
whole dried red chiles, broken into pieces	4	8	8
fresh curry leaves	7	14	20

1. Place the inner pot in your Instant Pot. Select the **SAUTE** setting and adjust to **MORE**. When the indicator flashes **HOT**, add the oil. Once the oil is hot, add the *hing*, turmeric, and dried chiles. *Because the oil pools to the sides, push the spices into the oil along the border of the inner pot so they can cook fully.*

2. Add the onions and fresh chiles. Stir and cook for 1 minute.

3. Add the tomatoes. Stir and cook for 1 minute.

4. Add the carrots, daikon, turnips, and potatoes. Stir and cook for 1 minute.

5. Press **CANCEL**. Add the *toor dal*, *sambhar* powder, red chile powder, salt, tamarind, and water. Stir. *NOTE: You can't add all the water to the 8-quart IP or you'll exceed the MAX Fill Line—you will add the remaining water after cooking.*

6. Lock the lid into place and make sure the pressure release valve is set to the sealing position (upwards). Press the **PRESSURE COOK** button and then press the **PRESSURE LEVEL** button until the panel reads **HIGH**. Adjust the time to cook to 8 minutes.

7. Once the cooking is complete, release the pressure naturally for 10 minutes. Then manually release the remaining pressure, press **CANCEL**, and remove the lid.

8. Prepare the *tarka* on the stovetop by warming the oil over medium-high heat in a shallow pan. Once the oil is hot, add the mustard seeds. Cook until the seeds pop and turn greyish, about 40 seconds. Add the dried chiles and curry leaves. *Keep a lid handy—the oil can splatter.* Stir and cook for 1 minute until the leaves wilt.

9. Carefully add this mixture to the Instant Pot. *The hot oil may splash once it hits the liquid.* For the 8-quart IP, add the remaining water. Stir and serve with *idli*, *dosa*, or plain rice. *All the spices are edible, including the curry leaves.*

SAMBHAR POWDER

YIELD: **1½ CUPS**

I have been blessed to grow up with South Indian family friends who have taught me how to cook, love, and appreciate South Indian dishes and spice blends like this *sambhar* powder. The absolute best *sambhars* are made with homemade blends. It's not hard at all! Make a batch and store it in an airtight container for up to 2 months.

½ cup firmly packed medium-large fresh curry leaves

1 cup dried red chiles

¼ cup coriander seeds

2 tablespoons cumin seeds

1 tablespoon fenugreek seeds

1 tablespoon black mustard seeds

1 tablespoon white poppy seeds

2 teaspoons *hing* (asafoetida)

2 (4-inch) cinnamon sticks, broken into pieces

1 tablespoon unrefined sesame or vegetable oil

¼ cup *chana dal* (dried, split, and skinned black chickpeas), picked over and washed

1. Combine all the spices in a bowl. Drizzle the oil over them and mix well.

2. Heat a skillet over medium-high heat. Add the *chana dal* and the spice mixture and cook, stirring constantly, until the curry leaves brown and curl up and the other spices brown, about 3 to 4 minutes.

3. Immediately transfer the mixture to a plate and cool for about 20 minutes. Once the mixture is cool, grind it in a coffee grinder reserved for spices. Store it in an airtight container for up to 2 months.

TRY THIS! Enjoy this powder sprinkled on popcorn for an Indian twist to family movie nights.

Lasan aur Lal Mirch Toor Dal

Garlic and Chile Split Pigeon Pea Curry

	3 QUART	6 QUART	8 QUART
Yield	5 cups	10 cups	15 cups
Warm up	10 mins	20 mins	20 mins
Cook	7 mins	7 mins	7 mins
Cool down	MR	MR	MR
Total time	roast + 17 mins	roast + 27 mins	roast + 27 mins

I wanted to add more flavor to the Instant Pot version of this recipe. It evolved into a drier take on Gujarati *Toor Dal*, but when you make it, you almost feel like it's a completely different dish. That's the beauty of Indian food. You can start with similar ingredients but end up with something very different.

Ingredients	3 QUART	6 QUART	8 QUART
cumin seeds	1 tsp	2 tsp	1 Tbsp
coriander seeds	1 tsp	2 tsp	1 Tbsp
oil or *ghee*	1 Tbsp	2 Tbsp	3 Tbsp
hing (asafoetida) (optional)	1 pinch	2 pinches	3 pinches
black mustard seeds	½ tsp	1 tsp	1½ tsp
whole cloves	3	6	9
cinnamon sticks	1 (1-inch)	1 (2-inch)	2 (2-inch)
turmeric powder	½ tsp	1 tsp	1½ tsp
whole dried red chiles, broken into pieces	4–6	6–8	6–8
yellow onion, minced	1 small	1 medium	1 medium
cloves of garlic, minced	2	4	4
fresh Thai or serrano chiles, stems removed and thinly sliced	1–3	2–6	8–10
tomatoes, diced	1 medium	2 medium	3 medium
light brown sugar	1 Tbsp	2 Tbsp	3 Tbsp
tamarind purée	1 Tbsp	2 Tbsp	3 Tbsp
salt	1 Tbsp	2 Tbsp	3 Tbsp
dhuli toor dal (dried, split, and skinned pigeon peas), picked over and washed (not soaked)	2 cups	4 cups	6 cups
water	3 cups	5 cups	7 cups
lemon juice	2 Tbsp	4 Tbsp	6 Tbsp

1. In a dry, shallow pan over medium-high heat, roast the cumin and coriander for 2 to 3 minutes until they turn reddish brown, shaking the pan a few times. Be careful not to burn them. Transfer to a dish to cool for 5 minutes and then grind to a fine powder with a mortar and pestle or in a coffee grinder reserved for spices. Set aside.

2. Place the inner pot in your Instant Pot. Select the **SAUTE** setting and adjust to **MORE**. When the indicator flashes **HOT**, add the oil. Once the oil is hot, add the *hing*, mustard, cloves, and cinnamon. Stir and cook for 2 minutes. *Because the oil pools to the sides, push the spices into the oil along the border of the inner pot so they can cook fully.*

3. Add the turmeric and dried chiles. Stir and cook for 30 seconds.

4. Add the onion. Stir and cook for 2 minutes.

5. Add the garlic and fresh chiles. Stir and cook for 30 seconds.

6. Add the tomatoes. Stir and cook for 1 minute.

7. Press **CANCEL**. Add the roasted cumin and coriander from Step 1, brown sugar, tamarind, and salt. Stir, breaking down the tamarind with the back of a spoon.

8. Add the *toor dal* and water. Stir again.

9. Lock the lid into place and make sure the pressure release valve is set to the sealing position (upwards). Press the **PRESSURE COOK** button until the panel reads **HIGH**. Adjust the cook time to 7 minutes.

10. Once the cooking is complete, release the pressure manually, press **CANCEL**, and remove the lid. Remove and discard the cinnamon sticks and the cloves or leave them in for flavor and eat around them. *All the other spices are edible.* Add the lemon juice and stir. Serve with plain basmati rice or Indian bread like *roti* or *naan*.

Chana Dal

Simple Split Black Chickpea Curry

Both my girls love this dish. There's something about the consistency of the *dal* (split and skinned black chickpeas) that makes them hearty but light at the same time. This is a good alternative to *toor dal*, which has a muskier taste and smell.

	3 QUART	6 QUART	8 QUART
Yield	8 cups	15½ cups	21 cups
Warm up	18 mins	27 mins	33 mins
Cook	15 mins	15 mins	15 mins
Cool down	10 mins NR + MR	10 mins NR + MR	10 mins NR + MR
Total time	soak + 43 mins + *tarka*	soak + 52 mins + *tarka*	soak + 58 mins + *tarka*

Ingredients for IP	3 QUART	6 QUART	8 QUART
chana dal (dried, split, and skinned black chickpeas), picked over and washed	2 cups	4 cups	6 cups
oil or *ghee*	1 Tbsp	2 Tbsp	3 Tbsp
hing (asafoetida) (optional)	1 pinch	2 pinches	3 pinches
cumin seeds	1 tsp	2 tsp	1 Tbsp
turmeric powder	½ tsp	1 tsp	1½ tsp
yellow or red onions, minced	1 small	1 medium	2 medium
piece of ginger, minced	1 (1-inch)	1 (2-inch)	1 (3-inch)
cloves of garlic, minced	2	4	6
fresh Thai or serrano chiles, stems removed and thinly sliced	1–3	2–6	4–8
tomatoes, puréed	1 small	1 medium	2 medium
ground coriander	1 Tbsp	2 Tbsp	3 Tbsp
red chile powder or cayenne pepper	1 Tbsp	2 Tbsp	3 Tbsp
salt	1 Tbsp	2 Tbsp	3 Tbsp
water, for cooking	5 cups	9 cups	13 cups
Ingredients for *tarka*	**3 QUART**	**6 QUART**	**8 QUART**
oil or *ghee*	1 tsp	2 tsp	1 Tbsp
red chile flakes	1 tsp	2 tsp	1 Tbsp

1. Soak the *chana dal* in ample boiled, hot water for 30 minutes or in room temperature water for 2 hours to overnight. Drain and discard the water.

2. Place the inner pot in your Instant Pot. Select the **SAUTE** setting and adjust to **MORE**. When the indicator flashes **HOT**, add the oil. Once the oil is hot, add the *hing* and cumin. Stir and cook for 1 minute until the seeds turn reddish brown. *Because the oil pools to the sides, push the spices into the oil so they fully cook.*

3. Add the turmeric. Stir and cook for 30 seconds.

4. Add the onions. Stir and cook for 3 minutes.

5. Add the ginger, garlic, and fresh chiles. Stir and cook for 1 minute.

6. Add the tomatoes. Stir and cook for 1 minute, scraping the bottom to loosen anything stuck.

7. Press **CANCEL**. Add the coriander, red chile powder, salt, *chana dal*, and cooking water. Stir.

8. Lock the lid into place. Make sure the pressure release valve is set to the sealing position (upwards). Press the **PRESSURE COOK** button and then press the **PRESSURE LEVEL** button until the panel reads **HIGH**. Adjust the cook time to 15 minutes.

9. Once the cooking is complete, release the pressure naturally for 10 minutes. Then manually release the remaining pressure, press **CANCEL**, and remove the lid.

10. Prepare the *tarka* on the stovetop by warming the oil over medium-high heat in a shallow pan. Once the oil is hot, add the red chile flakes and cook for about 40 seconds. Immediately add this to the *chana dal*. Use a potato masher or a whisk to break down some of the dal and thicken it up. All the spices are edible. Serve with basmati rice or on its own as a soup.

Moong Dal Chilkha Kitchari

Split Green Dal and Rice Porridge

In Indian households, if you have an upset stomach or just want something comforting to eat, we don't reach for the chicken noodle soup, we make *kitchari*. Simply translated, the word means "all mixed up." Make it a few times and your family may feign an upset stomach to get you to make it more often!

	3 QUART	6 QUART	8 QUART
Yield	7 cups	15 cups	23 cups
Warm up	19 mins	28 mins	29 mins
Cook	4 mins	4 mins	4 mins
Cool down	MR	MR	MR
Total time	23 mins	32 mins	33 mins

Ingredients	3 QUART	6 QUART	8 QUART
moong dal chilkha (dried, split green *dal* with skin), picked over (not soaked)	1 cup	2 cups	3 cups
uncooked white basmati rice	1 cup	2 cups	3 cups
oil or *ghee*	1 Tbsp	2 Tbsp	3 Tbsp
hing (asafoetida)	1 pinch	2 pinches	3 pinches
ajwain (carom seeds)	½ tsp	1 tsp	1½ tsp
turmeric powder	½ tsp	1 tsp	1½ tsp
piece of ginger, minced	1 (2-inch)	1 (4-inch)	1 (6-inch)
salt	2 tsp	1 Tbsp + 1 tsp	2 Tbsp
water, for cooking	6 cups	12 cups	16 cups
butter or *ghee*, for garnish	2 tsp	1 Tbsp	2 Tbsp

1. Mix the *moong dal* and rice together in a roomy bowl and rinse.

2. Place the inner pot in your Instant Pot. Select the **SAUTE** setting and adjust to **NORMAL**. When the indicator flashes **HOT**, add the oil. Once the oil is hot, add the *hing*, *ajwain*, and turmeric. Stir and cook for 40 seconds until the seeds turn reddish brown. *Because the oil pools to the sides, push the spices into the oil so they fully cook.*

3. Add the ginger. Stir and cook for 30 seconds.

4. Press **CANCEL**. Add the *dal* and rice mixture, salt, and cooking water. Stir.

5. Lock the lid into place and make sure the pressure release valve is set to the sealing position (upwards). Press the **PRESSURE COOK** button and then press the **PRESSURE LEVEL** button until the panel reads **HIGH**. Adjust the cook time to 4 minutes.

6. Once the cooking is complete, release the pressure manually, press **CANCEL**, and remove the lid. Add the butter and serve steaming hot with a dollop of *achaar* (Indian pickle). Add sliced onion and fresh green chiles for an added crunch and layer of texture and flavor. *All the spices are edible.*

Sabut Moong Kitchari

Whole Green *Dal* and Brown Rice Porridge

From the moment my girls could eat rice, I fed them brown rather than white. They eventually developed a taste for the whole-grain version. Cooked in an Instant Pot with *dal*, brown rice cooks surprisingly quickly, tastes delicious, and is the perfect hearty backdrop for this dish.

	3 QUART	6 QUART	8 QUART
Yield	7 cups	15 cups	23 cups
Warm up	18 mins	27 mins	30 mins
Cook	12 mins	12 mins	12 mins
Cool down	MR	MR	MR
Total time	soak + 30 mins	soak + 39 mins	soak + 42 mins

Ingredients	3 QUART	6 QUART	8 QUART
sabut moong dal (whole, dried green *dal* with skin), picked over and washed	1½ cups	3 cups	5 cups
uncooked brown rice	½ cup	1 cup	2½ cups
oil or *ghee*	1 Tbsp	2 Tbsp	3 Tbsp
hing (asafoetida) (optional)	1 pinch	2 pinches	3 pinches
cumin seeds	2 tsp	1 Tbsp + 1 tsp	2 Tbsp
turmeric powder	½ tsp	1 tsp	2 tsp
yellow or red onions, minced	1 small	1 medium	2 medium
piece of ginger, minced	1 (1-inch)	1 (2-inch)	1 (3-inch)
cloves of garlic, minced	2	4	6
fresh Thai or serrano chiles, stems removed, thinly sliced	1–3	2–6	3–7
garam masala	1 tsp	2 tsp	1 Tbsp
red chile powder or cayenne pepper	1 tsp	2 tsp	1 Tbsp
salt	1 Tbsp	2 Tbsp	2 Tbsp + 2 tsp
water, for cooking	6 cups	12 cups	16 cups
finely chopped fresh cilantro, for garnish	1 Tbsp	2 Tbsp	3 Tbsp
minced yellow, red, or white onion, for garnish	2 Tbsp	¼ cup	½ cup
butter or *ghee*, for garnish	2 tsp	1 Tbsp + 1 tsp	2 Tbsp

1. Mix the *moong dal* and rice together in a roomy bowl and soak in ample boiled, hot water for 20 minutes or in room temperature water for 2 hours to overnight. Drain and discard the water.

2. Place the inner pot in your Instant Pot. Select the **SAUTE** setting and adjust to **MORE**. When the indicator flashes **HOT**, add the oil. Once the oil is hot, add the *hing* and cumin. Stir and cook for 40 seconds until the seeds turn reddish brown. *Because the oil pools to the sides, push the spices into the oil so they fully cook.*

3. Add the turmeric. Stir and cook for 30 seconds.

4. Add the onions. Stir and cook for 1 minute.

5. Add the ginger, garlic, and fresh chiles. Stir and cook for 1 minute.

6. Press **CANCEL**. Add the *garam masala*, red chile powder, salt, *moong*-rice mixture, and cooking water. Stir.

7. Lock the lid into place and make sure the pressure release valve is set to the sealing position (upwards). Press the **PRESSURE COOK** button and then press the **PRESSURE LEVEL** button until the panel reads **HIGH**. Adjust the cook time to 12 minutes.

8. Once the cooking is complete, release the pressure manually, press **CANCEL**, and remove the lid. Add the cilantro, onion, and *ghee*. For even more flavor, add a dollop of *achaar* (Indian pickle). Eat steaming hot alone or with a brothy, spicy curry on the side. *All the spices are edible.*

Sookhi Dal

Dry Spiced *Dal*

This is one of my husband's favorite dishes. It's a good thing I figured out how to make it in the Instant Pot. The key, because it is a dry dish, is to use the pot-in-pot cooking method. This way it comes out perfect every time and you avoid the dreaded burn warning no matter which size pressure cooker you use.

	3 QUART	6 QUART	8 QUART
Yield	6 cups	12 cups	15 cups
Warm up	12 mins	19 mins	9 mins
Cook	6 mins	6 mins	6 mins
Cool down	10 mins NR + MR	10 mins NR + MR	10 mins NR + MR
Total time	28 mins	35 mins	25 mins

Ingredients	3 QUART	6 QUART	8 QUART
oil or *ghee*	1 Tbsp	2 Tbsp	3 Tbsp
hing (asafoetida) (optional)	1 pinch	2 pinches	3 pinches
cumin seeds	2 tsp	1 Tbsp + 1 tsp	2 Tbsp
turmeric powder	½ tsp	1 tsp	1½ tsp
yellow or red onions, minced	1 small	1 medium	2 medium
piece of ginger, minced	1 (1-inch)	1 (2-inch)	1 (3-inch)
cloves of garlic, minced	2	4	6
fresh Thai or serrano chiles, stems removed, thinly sliced	1–4	2–8	3–9
tomatoes, diced	1 small	1 medium	2 medium
garam masala	2 tsp	1 Tbsp + 1 tsp	2 Tbsp
amchur (dried mango powder)	2 tsp	1 Tbsp + 1 tsp	2 Tbsp
red chile powder or cayenne pepper	2 tsp	1 Tbsp + 1 tsp	2 Tbsp
salt	2 tsp	1 Tbsp + 1 tsp	2 Tbsp
water, plus more for pot-in-pot cooking	2 cups	4 cups	6 cups
dhuli moong dal (dried, split, and skinned yellow *moong*) or *dhuli urad dal* (dried, split, and skinned black *dal*), picked over and washed (not soaked)	2 cups	4 cups	6 cups
lemon juice	½ lemon	1 lemon	1½ lemons
minced fresh cilantro, for garnish	2 Tbsp	¼ cup	¾ cup

1. Place the inner pot in your Instant Pot. Select the **SAUTE** setting and adjust to **MORE**. When the indicator flashes **HOT**, add the oil. When the oil is hot, add the *hing* and cumin. Stir and cook for 1 minute until the seeds turn reddish brown. *Because the oil pools to the sides, push the spices into the oil along the border of the inner pot so they cook fully.*

2. Add the turmeric. Stir and cook for 40 seconds.

3. Add the onions. Stir and cook for 1 minute.

4. Add the ginger, garlic, and fresh chiles. Stir and cook for 30 seconds.

5. Press **CANCEL**. Carefully move the inner pot to a heat-resistant surface and transfer the mixture to an oven-safe glass or metal bowl, scraping the bottom to loosen anything stuck. *Add a little water if needed to deglaze the pot. The bowl must fit in the Instant Pot with the lid on for pot-in-pot cooking.*

6. Into the same bowl, add the tomatoes, *garam masala*, *amchur*, red chile powder, salt, and water and stir. Add the *moong dal* and stir again.

7. Return the empty inner pot to the base, pour in some additional water (1 cup for a 3-quart IP, 2 cups for 6-quart IP, 3 cups for an 8-quart IP), position a trivet in the pot, and place the bowl from Step 6 on the trivet.

8. Lock the lid into place. Make sure that the pressure release valve is set to the sealing position (upwards). Press the **PRESSURE COOK** button and then press the **PRESSURE LEVEL** button until the panel reads **LOW**. Adjust the cook time to 6 minutes.

9. Once the cooking is complete, release the pressure naturally for 10 minutes. Then manually release the remaining pressure, press **CANCEL**, and remove the lid. Add the lemon juice and garnish with the cilantro. Serve with Indian bread like *roti* or *naan*, stuffed in a pita, as a side salad with greens, or paired with a grilled protein or vegetables. *All the spices are edible.*

Rajmah

Punjabi Curried Kidney Beans

Ah, *rajmah*! This is the ultimate Punjabi dish—the North Indian version of chili or red beans and rice. It is the quintessential comfort food for Punjabis. Ask anyone from that region, and they will tell you they grew up eating these hearty beans over rice at home for a weekend lunch or in their college cafeteria.

	3 QUART	6 QUART	8 QUART
Yield	6 cups	12 cups	17 cups
Warm up	17 mins	28 mins	27 mins
Cook	35 mins	35 mins	35 mins
Cool down	10 mins NR + MR	10 mins NR + MR	10 mins NR + MR
Total time	soak + 62 mins	soak + 73 mins	soak + 72 mins

Ingredients	3 QUART	6 QUART	8 QUART
rajmah (dried red kidney beans), picked over and washed	2 cups	4 cups	6 cups
oil or *ghee*	1 Tbsp	2 Tbsp	3 Tbsp
hing (asafoetida) (optional)	1 pinch	2 pinches	3 pinches
cumin seeds	2 tsp	1 Tbsp	1 Tbsp + 1 tsp
turmeric powder	1 tsp	2 tsp	2½ tsp
whole cloves	4	6	8
cinnamon sticks	1 (2-inch)	1 (2-inch)	2 (2-inch)
black cardamom pods	1	2	3
yellow or red onions, minced	1 small	1 medium	2 medium
piece of ginger, minced	1 (1-inch)	1 (2-inch)	1 (3-inch)
cloves of garlic, minced	2	4	6
fresh Thai or serrano chiles, stems removed, thinly sliced	1–4	2–8	3–10
tomatoes, diced or puréed	1 small	1 medium	2 medium
unsalted tomato paste	2 Tbsp	¼ cup	⅔ cup
garam masala	1 Tbsp	2 Tbsp	2 Tbsp + 1 tsp
ground coriander	1 Tbsp	2 Tbsp	2 Tbsp + 1 tsp
amchur (dried mango powder)	1 Tbsp	2 Tbsp	2 Tbsp + 1 tsp
red chile powder or cayenne pepper	2 tsp	1 Tbsp	1 Tbsp + 1 tsp
salt	1 Tbsp	2 Tbsp	3 Tbsp
water, for cooking	3 cups	6 cups	8 cups
chopped fresh cilantro, for garnish	1 Tbsp	2 Tbsp	¼ cup

1. Soak the *rajmah* in ample boiled, hot water for at least 1 hour or in room temperature water for 6 hours to overnight. Drain and discard the water.

2. Place the inner pot in your Instant Pot. Select the **SAUTE** setting and adjust to **MORE**. When the indicator flashes **HOT**, add the oil. Once the oil is hot, add the *hing* and cumin. Stir and cook for 40 seconds until the seeds turn reddish brown. *Because the oil pools to the sides, push the spices into the oil along the border of the inner pot so they can cook fully.*

3. Add the turmeric. Stir and cook for 30 seconds.

4. Add the cloves, cinnamon, and cardamom. Stir and cook for 30 seconds.

5. Add the onions. Stir and cook for 1 minute.

6. Add the ginger, garlic, and fresh chiles. Stir and cook for 1 minute.

7. Press **CANCEL**. Add the tomatoes, tomato paste, *garam masala*, coriander, *amchur*, red chile powder, salt, *rajmah*, and cooking water. Stir.

8. Lock the lid into place and make sure the pressure release valve is set to the sealing position (upwards). Press the **PRESSURE COOK** button and then press the **PRESSURE LEVEL** button until the panel reads **HIGH**. Adjust the cook time to 35 minutes.

9. Once the cooking is complete, release the pressure naturally for 10 minutes. Then manually release the remaining pressure, press **CANCEL**, and remove the lid. Remove and discard the cloves, cinnamon, and cardamom or leave them in for flavor and eat around them. *All the other spices are edible.* Mash some of the beans with the back of a spatula. Add the cilantro and serve over basmati rice with a side of *raita* (spiced yogurt) and onion. *If you prefer the beans to break down even more, increase the cook time by 5 to 10 minutes.*

Dad's *Rajmah*

Since I introduced this recipe in *The Indian Slow Cooker*, hundreds of fans have emailed me thanking my dad for his recipe. He loves the feedback! While this recipe is like the previous *rajmah*, it is simpler—there are no fancy spices, but the butter makes up for it.

	3 QUART	6 QUART	8 QUART
Yield	6 cups	12 cups	17 cups
Warm up	17 mins	26 mins	27 mins
Cook	35 mins	35 mins	35 mins
Cool down	10 mins NR + MR	10 mins NR + MR	10 mins NR + MR
Total time	soak + 62 mins	soak + 71 mins	soak + 72 mins

Ingredients	3 QUART	6 QUART	8 QUART
rajmah (dried red kidney beans), picked over and washed	2 cups	4 cups	6 cups
unsalted butter or *ghee*	3 Tbsp	6 Tbsp	8 Tbsp
cumin seeds	2 tsp	1 Tbsp	1 Tbsp + 1 tsp
turmeric powder	1 tsp	2 tsp	2 tsp
yellow or red onions, minced	1 small	1 medium	2 medium
piece of ginger, minced	1 (2-inch)	1 (4-inch)	1 (6-inch)
cloves of garlic, minced	10	20	30
fresh Thai or serrano chiles, stems removed, thinly sliced	8–10	16–20	20–25
unsalted tomato paste	¼ cup	½ cup	⅔ cup
red chile powder or cayenne pepper	2 tsp	1 Tbsp + 1 tsp	2 Tbsp
salt	1 Tbsp + 1 tsp	2 Tbsp + 2 tsp	3 Tbsp
water, for cooking	3 cups	6 cups	8 cups
chopped fresh cilantro, for garnish	1 Tbsp	2 Tbsp	¼ cup

1. Soak the *rajmah* in ample boiled, hot water for at least 1 hour or in room temperature water for 6 hours to overnight. Drain and discard the water.

2. Place the inner pot in your Instant Pot. Select the **SAUTE** setting and adjust to **MORE**. When the indicator flashes **HOT**, add the butter, cumin, and turmeric. Stir and cook for 1 minute.

3. Add the onions. Stir and cook for 2 minutes.

4. Add the ginger, garlic, and fresh chiles. Stir and cook for 1 minute.

5. Press **CANCEL**. Add the tomato paste, red chile powder, salt, *rajmah*, and cooking water and stir.

6. Lock the lid into place and make sure the pressure release valve is set to the sealing position (upwards). Press the **PRESSURE COOK** button and then press the **PRESSURE LEVEL** button until the panel reads **HIGH**. Adjust the cook time to 35 minutes.

7. Once the cooking is complete, release the pressure naturally for 10 minutes. Then manually release the remaining pressure, press **CANCEL**, and remove the lid. Garnish with the cilantro and serve over plain basmati rice with a side of *raita* (spiced yogurt) and onion. *All the spices are edible.*

Chana Masala

Curried Chickpeas

Like *rajmah*, this dish is a staple in virtually every North Indian home. It's a delicious and hearty non-meat protein alternative for many Indians—vegetarians and meat eaters alike. This Instant Pot recipe is a little brothier than the slow-cooked version, and it could not make me happier.

	3 QUART	6 QUART	8 QUART
Yield	6 cups	12 cups	17 cups
Warm up	13 mins	25 mins	30 mins
Cook	30 mins	30 mins	30 mins
Cool down	10 mins NR + MR	10 mins NR + MR	10 mins NR + MR
Total time	soak + 53 mins	soak + 65 mins	soak + 70 mins

Ingredients	3 QUART	6 QUART	8 QUART
kabuli chana (dried white chickpeas), picked over and washed	2 cups	4 cups	6 cups
oil or *ghee*	1 Tbsp	2 Tbsp	3 Tbsp
hing (asafoetida) (optional)	1 pinch	2 pinches	3 pinches
cumin seeds	2 tsp	1 Tbsp	1 Tbsp + 2 tsp
turmeric powder	1 tsp	2 tsp	1 Tbsp
yellow or red onions, minced	1 small	1 medium	2 medium
piece of ginger, minced	1 (1-inch)	1 (2-inch)	1 (3-inch)
cloves of garlic, minced	2	4	6
fresh Thai or serrano chiles, stems removed, thinly sliced	1–4	2–8	3–9
tomatoes, puréed	1 small	1 medium	2 medium
unsalted tomato paste	1 Tbsp	2 Tbsp	3 Tbsp
garam masala	2 tsp	1 Tbsp + 1 tsp	2 Tbsp
ground coriander	2 tsp	1 Tbsp + 1 tsp	2 Tbsp
red chile powder or cayenne pepper	2 tsp	1 Tbsp + 1 tsp	2 Tbsp
chana masala (see recipe on page 83)	1 Tbsp	2 Tbsp	3 Tbsp
salt	1 Tbsp	2 Tbsp	3 Tbsp
water, for cooking	3 cups	6 cups	9 cups
chopped fresh cilantro, for garnish	1 Tbsp	2 Tbsp	¼ cup

1. Soak the *chana* in ample boiled, hot water for at least 1 hour or in room temperature water for 6 hours to overnight. Drain and discard the water.

2. Place the inner pot in your Instant Pot. Select the **SAUTE** setting and adjust to **MORE**. When the indicator flashes **HOT**, add the oil. Once the oil is hot, add the *hing* and cumin. Stir and cook for 1 minute until the seeds turn reddish brown. *Because the oil pools to the sides, push the spices into the oil along the border of the pot so they can cook fully.*

3. Add the turmeric. Stir and cook for 30 seconds.

4. Add the onions. Stir and cook for 1 minute for a 3-quart IP or up to 3 minutes for a 6-quart or 8-quart IP.

5. Add the ginger, garlic, and fresh chiles. Stir and cook for 1 minute.

6. Press **CANCEL**. Add the tomatoes, tomato paste, *garam masala*, coriander, red chile powder, *chana masala*, salt, *chana*, and cooking water. Stir.

7. Lock the lid into place and make sure the pressure release valve is set to the sealing position (upwards). Press the **PRESSURE COOK** button and then press the **PRESSURE LEVEL** button until the panel reads **HIGH**. Adjust the cook time to 30 minutes.

8. Once the cooking is complete, release the pressure naturally for 10 minutes. Then manually release the remaining pressure, press **CANCEL**, and remove the lid. Garnish with the cilantro and serve over basmati rice or with Indian bread like *roti* or *naan*. *If you want to thicken this up, break down some of the chickpeas with the back of a spoon or an immersion blender. All the spices are edible.*

TRY THIS! Toast a hamburger bun. Place a slice of cheese (any kind) on each half of the bun and heap on a spoonful of *chana* and fresh, diced onions. It's a fast and healthy veggie alternative to the open-faced sandwich.

CHANA (CHOLE, CHOLAY) MASALA

YIELD: **1½ CUPS**

This is the perfect spice blend for the spicy chickpea curry called *chana masala.* (It's a little confusing, but the dish and the spice blend go by the same name.) The key to this spice blend is the dried pomegranate seeds, which lend a needed sourness to the dish. Sheer perfection!

¼ cup cumin seeds

¼ cup coriander seeds

¼ cup *anardana* (dried pomegranate seeds)

2 teaspoons black mustard seeds

2 teaspoons fenugreek seeds

10 whole cloves

2 black cardamom pods

4 green cardamom pods

3 (3-inch) cinnamon sticks, broken into pieces

1 teaspoon *ajwain* (carom seeds)

1 tablespoon whole black peppercorns

5 medium cassia leaves or bay leaves, broken into pieces

10 whole dried red chiles, broken into pieces

1 tablespoon *kasoori methi* (dried fenugreek leaves), lightly hand crushed to release flavor

2 tablespoons *amchur* (dried mango powder)

1 tablespoon ground ginger

1 tablespoon *kala namak* (black salt)

1. In a shallow, heavy pan, dry roast the cumin, coriander, pomegranate seeds, mustard, fenugreek seeds, cloves, black and green cardamom pods, cinnamon, carom, peppercorns, cassia or bay leaves, red chiles, and fenugreek leaves over medium heat. Stay close, and shake the pan every 15 to 20 seconds to prevent the spices from burning. They should be just toasted and aromatic. After about 4 minutes of roasting, transfer the mixture to a plate and allow it to cool for 15 minutes.

2. Once the mixture is cool, transfer it to a spice grinder or the dry jug of a powerful blender. Add the *amchur*, ginger, and *kala namak* and process to a fine powder. You may need to grind it in small batches, depending on the size of your grinder. Sift after grinding to get a finer powder. Store in an airtight container for up to 6 months.

Sookha Amla Chana

Amla Chickpeas

My mom showed me how to make this dry *chana* dish and I can't stop making it—it's so delicious. The key is to darken the chickpeas during the cooking process using dried *amla*, an Indian gooseberry. Any well-stocked Indian grocer will carry *amla*, but if you can't find it, just use black tea bags.

	3 QUART	6 QUART	8 QUART
Yield	5½ cups	10 cups	16 cups
Warm up	10 mins	14 mins	16 mins
Cook	35 mins	35 mins	35 mins
Cool down	10 mins NR + MR	10 mins NR + MR	10 mins NR + MR
Total time	soak + 55 mins + *tarka*	soak + 59 mins + *tarka*	soak + 61 mins + *tarka*

Ingredients for IP	3 QUART	6 QUART	8 QUART
kabuli chana (dried white chickpeas), picked over and washed	2 cups	4 cups	6 cups
pieces of dried whole *amla* (or black tea bags, tags removed, leave the strings on)	6 (or 1)	12 (or 2)	15 (or 3)
water, for cooking	1 cup	2 cups	3 cups

Ingredients for *tarka*	3 QUART	6 QUART	8 QUART
yellow or red onion, thinly sliced lengthwise	½ cup	1 cup	2 cups
tomatoes, sliced lengthwise	1 small	1 medium	2 medium
piece of ginger, cut into thin, 1-inch matchsticks	1 (1-inch)	1 (2-inch)	1 (3-inch)
cloves of garlic, minced	1	2	3
fresh Thai or serrano chiles, stems removed and sliced lengthwise	2–4	4–8	5–10
chana masala (see recipe on page 83)	1 Tbsp	2 Tbsp	3 Tbsp
red chile powder or cayenne pepper	1 tsp	2 tsp	1 Tbsp
salt	1 Tbsp	2 Tbsp	3 Tbsp
turmeric powder	½ tsp	1 tsp	2 tsp
cumin seeds	1 tsp	2 tsp	1 Tbsp
vegetable oil	¼ cup	⅓ cup	⅓ cup
lemon juice	½ lemon	1 lemon	1½ lemons
chopped fresh cilantro, for garnish	2 Tbsp	3 Tbsp	¼ cup

1. Soak the *chana* in ample boiled, hot water for 1 hour or in room temperature water for 6 hours to overnight. Drain and discard the water.

2. Place the inner pot in your Instant Pot. Add the *chana*, *amla* or teabags, and cooking water in that order.

3. Lock the lid into place and make sure the pressure release valve is set to the sealing position (upwards). Press the **PRESSURE COOK** button and then press the **PRESSURE LEVEL** button until the panel reads **HIGH**. Adjust the cook time to 35 minutes.

4. Once the cooking is complete, release the pressure naturally for 10 minutes. Then manually release the remaining pressure, press **CANCEL**, and remove the lid. Remove and discard the tea bag if using. If using *amla*, leave it in—it's healthy to eat.

5. With a spoon, make a shallow well in the middle of the *chana*. In it, add the onion, tomatoes, ginger, garlic, fresh chiles, *chana masala*, red chile powder, salt, turmeric, and cumin in that order. *The order is important—the cumin should be on top.*

6. On the stovetop, warm the oil in a shallow pan over medium-high heat until it just starts to smoke. *The oil must be very hot but be careful it does not burn. Test it by dropping in a single cumin seed, and if it sizzles immediately, the oil is ready.* Working slowly, pour the oil over the fresh ingredients in the Instant Pot. *As it hits the cumin seeds, they will sizzle and cook.*

7. Add the lemon juice and stir until all the spices and ingredients are mixed evenly. Garnish with the cilantro and serve with Indian bread like *roti* or *naan* or stuffed in a pita and drizzled with *raita* (spiced yogurt) or tamarind or mint chutney. *All the spices are edible. The chickpeas will be al dente. If you prefer them softer, increase the cook time by 5 minutes.*

NOTE: There have been times when I've had to refrigerate the plain, cooked chickpeas and finish them off later. If this is the case, reheat the beans first either on the stovetop or in the Instant Pot using the SAUTE setting, adding a little water so they don't stick. If you add the garnish and hot oil on cold beans, it won't pull together the same way.

Khata Imlee Chana

Tangy Tamarind Chickpeas

The tartness of this dish takes me back to eating freshly seasoned and spiced chickpeas along the lake in Chandigarh, India, the city where I was born and spent much of my childhood visiting. Back then, my *nani* forbade us to eat street food, but my cousins and I always snuck out of the house to get our fill.

	3 QUART	6 QUART	8 QUART
Yield	7 cups	11 cups	16 cups
Warm up	13 mins	25 mins	29 mins
Cook	40 mins	40 mins	40 mins
Cool down	10 mins NR + MR	10 mins NR + MR	10 mins NR + MR
Total time	soak + 63 mins	soak + 75 mins	soak + 79 mins

Ingredients	3 QUART	6 QUART	8 QUART
kabuli chana (dried white chickpeas), picked over and washed	2 cups	4 cups	6 cups
vegetable oil	1 Tbsp	2 Tbsp	3 Tbsp
hing (asafoetida) (optional)	1 pinch	2 pinches	3 pinches
yellow or red onions, puréed	1 small	1 medium	2 medium
piece of ginger, puréed	1 (1-inch)	1 (2-inch)	1 (3-inch)
cloves of garlic, puréed	8	16	20
fresh Thai or serrano chiles, stems removed, thinly sliced	2–4	4–8	5–10
tamarind purée	2 Tbsp	¼ cup	¼ cup + 2 Tbsp
plain, unsweetened *hung curd* or Greek yogurt	¼ cup	½ cup	¾ cup
ground cumin	1 Tbsp	2 Tbsp	3 Tbsp
ground coriander	1 Tbsp	2 Tbsp	3 Tbsp
garam masala	1 Tbsp	2 Tbsp	3 Tbsp
red chile powder or cayenne pepper	1 Tbsp	2 Tbsp	3 Tbsp
salt	1 Tbsp	2 Tbsp	3 Tbsp
water, for cooking	3 cups	5 cups	7 cups
lemon juice	½ lemon	1 lemon	1½ lemons
yellow or red onions, sliced in thin rounds, for garnish	1 small	1 medium	2 medium

1. Soak the *chana* in ample boiled, hot water for at least 1 hour or in room temperature water for 6 hours to overnight. Drain and discard the water.

2. Place the inner pot in your Instant Pot. Select the **SAUTE** setting and adjust to **MORE**. When the indicator flashes **HOT**, add the oil. Once the oil is hot, add the *hing* and puréed onions. Stir and cook for 3 minutes.

3. Add the ginger, garlic, and fresh chiles. Stir and cook for 2 minutes. *If this starts sticking, add 2 tablespoons of water.*

4. Add the tamarind. Stir and cook for 1 minute.

5. Press **CANCEL**. Add the yogurt, cumin, coriander, *garam masala*, red chile powder, salt, *chana*, and cooking water. Stir.

6. Lock the lid into place and make sure the pressure release valve is set to the sealing position (upwards). Press the **PRESSURE COOK** button and then press the **PRESSURE LEVEL** button until the panel reads **HIGH**. Adjust the cook time to 40 minutes.

7. Once the cooking is complete, release the pressure naturally for 10 minutes. Then manually release the remaining pressure, press **CANCEL**, and remove the lid. Add the lemon juice and stir. Garnish with the fresh onion rounds and serve with basmati rice or with Indian bread like *roti*, *naan*, or *puri*. *All the spices are edible.*

Kala Chana

Black Chickpea Curry

These chickpeas are nothing like their white counterparts. They are smaller, brownish black in color, and extremely thick-skinned. They have a warm, earthy flavor that I sometimes prefer over white chickpeas. The Instant Pot is the perfect way to cook these chickpeas quickly while still locking in all the delicious flavor.

	3 QUART	6 QUART	8 QUART
Yield	8 cups	15 cups	20 cups
Warm up	19 mins	32 mins	34 mins
Cook	35 mins	35 mins	35 mins
Cool down	10 mins NR + MR	10 mins NR + MR	10 mins NR + MR
Total time	soak + 64 mins	soak + 77 mins	soak + 79 mins

Ingredients	3 QUART	6 QUART	8 QUART
kala chana (dried whole black chickpeas), picked over and washed	2 cups	4 cups	6 cups
oil or ghee	1 Tbsp	2 Tbsp	3 Tbsp
hing (asafoetida) (optional)	1 pinch	2 pinches	3 pinches
cumin seeds	2 tsp	1 Tbsp + 1 tsp	1 Tbsp + 2 tsp
turmeric powder	1 tsp	2 tsp	1 Tbsp
yellow or red onions, minced	1 small	1 medium	2 medium
piece of ginger, minced	1 (1-inch)	1 (2-inch)	1 (3-inch)
cloves of garlic, minced	3	6	8
fresh Thai or serrano chiles, stems removed, thinly sliced	1–6	2–12	3–13
tomatoes, diced or puréed	1 small	1 medium	2 medium
unsalted tomato paste	2 Tbsp	¼ cup	⅔ cup
garam masala	1 Tbsp	2 Tbsp	3 Tbsp
red chile powder or cayenne pepper	2 tsp	1 Tbsp	2 Tbsp
salt	1 Tbsp	2 Tbsp	3 Tbsp
water, for cooking	4 cups	8 cups	11 cups
lemon juice	2 Tbsp	3 Tbsp	¼ cup
chopped fresh cilantro, for garnish	2 Tbsp	¼ cup	⅔ cup

1. Soak the *chana* in ample boiled, hot water for at least 1 hour or in room temperature water for 6 hours to overnight. Drain and discard the water.

2. Place the inner pot in your Instant Pot. Select the **SAUTE** setting and adjust to **MORE**. When the indicator flashes **HOT**, add the oil. Once the oil is hot, add the *hing* and cumin. Stir and cook for 1 minute until the seeds turn reddish brown. *Because the oil pools to the sides, push the spices into the oil along the border of the inner pot so they can cook fully.*

3. Add the turmeric. Stir and cook for 30 seconds.

4. Add the onions. Stir and cook for 1 minute.

5. Add the ginger, garlic, and fresh chiles. Stir and cook for 1 minute.

6. Press **CANCEL**. Add the tomatoes, tomato paste, *garam masala*, red chile powder, salt, *chana*, and cooking water. Stir.

7. Lock the lid into place and make sure the pressure release valve is set to the sealing position (upwards). Press the **PRESSURE COOK** button and then press the **PRESSURE LEVEL** button until the panel reads **HIGH**. Adjust the cook time to 35 minutes.

8. Once the cooking is complete, release the pressure naturally for 10 minutes. Then manually release the remaining pressure, press **CANCEL**, and remove the lid. Add the lemon juice and stir. Garnish with the cilantro and serve with basmati rice or eat with Indian bread like *puri. All the spices are edible.*

Sookha Khata Kala Chana

Dry, Tangy Black Chickpeas

There are hundreds of Hindu festivals, and just as many special foods associated with them. Dried, spicy, sour, black chickpeas are considered especially auspicious when eaten with fried *puris* and sweet *halwa*. To make this dish in the Instant Pot, you only need a very small amount of water to just cook the chickpeas through.

	3 QUART	6 QUART	8 QUART
Yield	5 cups	10 cups	16 cups
Warm up	11 mins	16 mins	20 mins
Cook	35 mins	35 mins	35 mins
Cool down	10 mins NR + MR	10 mins NR + MR	10 mins NR + MR
Total time	soak + 56 mins	soak + 61 mins	soak + 65 mins

Ingredients	3 QUART	6 QUART	8 QUART
kala chana (dried whole black chickpeas), picked over and washed	2 cups	4 cups	6 cups
oil or *ghee*	1 Tbsp	2 Tbsp	3 Tbsp
hing (asafoetida) (optional)	1 pinch	2 pinches	3 pinches
shyah jeera (caraway seeds) or cumin seeds	2 tsp	1 Tbsp + 1 tsp	2 Tbsp
black cardamom pods	1	2	3
turmeric powder	½ tsp	1 tsp	1½ tsp
yellow or red onions, minced	1 small	1 medium	2 medium
piece of ginger, minced	1 (1-inch)	1 (2-inch)	1 (3-inch)
cloves of garlic, minced	2	4	6
fresh Thai or serrano chiles, stems removed, thinly sliced	1–4	2–8	3–10
tomatoes, diced	1 small	1 medium	2 medium
garam masala	1 Tbsp	2 Tbsp	3 Tbsp
amchur (dried mango powder)	1 Tbsp	2 Tbsp	3 Tbsp
red chile powder or cayenne pepper	1 Tbsp	2 Tbsp	3 Tbsp
salt	1 Tbsp	2 Tbsp	3 Tbsp
water, for cooking	½ cup	1 cup	1½ cups
lemon juice	½ lemon	1 lemon	1½ lemons
chopped fresh cilantro, for garnish	2 Tbsp	3 Tbsp	¼ cup

1. Soak the *chana* in ample boiled, hot water for at least 1 hour or in room temperature water for 6 hours to overnight. Drain and discard the water.

2. Place the inner pot in your Instant Pot. Select the **SAUTE** setting and adjust to **MORE**. When the indicator flashes **HOT**, add the oil. Once the oil is hot, add the *hing*, *shyah jeera* or cumin, and cardamom. Stir and cook for 1 minute until the seeds turn reddish brown. *Because the oil pools to the sides, push the spices into the oil along the border of the inner pot so they can cook fully.*

3. Add the turmeric. Stir and cook for 30 seconds.

4. Add the onions. Stir and cook for 2 minutes.

5. Add the ginger, garlic, and fresh chiles. Stir and cook for 1 minute.

6. Add the tomatoes. Cook for 1 minute and stir, scraping the bottom of the pot to loosen anything stuck.

7. Press **CANCEL**. Add the *garam masala*, *amchur*, red chile powder, salt, *chana*, and cooking water. Stir.

8. Lock the lid into place and make sure the pressure release valve is set to the sealing position (upwards). Press the **PRESSURE COOK** button and then press the **PRESSURE LEVEL** button until the panel reads **HIGH**. Adjust the cook time to 35 minutes.

9. Once the cooking is complete, release the pressure naturally for 10 minutes. Then manually release the remaining pressure, press **CANCEL**, and remove the lid. Remove and discard the cardamom or leave it in for flavor and eat around it. *All the other spices are edible.* Add the lemon juice and stir. Garnish with the cilantro and serve with Indian bread like *puri*, *roti*, or *naan*. This is also delicious as a side salad topped with a dollop of sweet tamarind chutney.

Kala Chana Sundal

Black Chickpeas with Coconut

Sundal is a delicious South Indian dish served in parks, temples, and beachside. You can make it with any legume, but it's typically made with black chickpeas. In this recipe *dal* is toasted, ground down, and used as a spice to give the dish additional layers of flavor. Serve it up warm or cold—both are delicious.

	3 QUART	6 QUART	8 QUART
Yield	6 cups	11 cups	17 cups
Warm up	10 mins	15 mins	19 mins
Cook	35 mins	35 mins	35 mins
Cool down	10 mins NR + MR	10 mins NR + MR	10 mins NR + MR
Total time	soak + roast + 55 mins	soak + roast + 60 mins	soak + roast + 64 mins

Ingredients	3 QUART	6 QUART	8 QUART
kala chana (dried whole black chickpeas), picked over and washed	2 cups	4 cups	6 cups
water, for cooking	½ cup	1 cup	1½ cups
dhuli urad dal (dried, split, and skinned black *dal*), picked over and washed (not soaked)	2 tsp	1 Tbsp + 1 tsp	2 Tbsp
chana dal (dried, split, and skinned black chickpeas), picked over and washed (not soaked)	2 tsp	1 Tbsp + 1 tsp	2 Tbsp
whole dried red chiles, broken into pieces	6	12	15
coriander seeds	2 tsp	1 Tbsp + 1 tsp	2 Tbsp
vegetable oil	1 Tbsp	2 Tbsp	3 Tbsp
hing (asafoetida)	1 pinch	2 pinches	3 pinches
black mustard seeds	1 tsp	2 tsp	1 Tbsp + 2 tsp
fresh curry leaves	12–15	15–20	20–25
fresh Thai or serrano chiles, stems removed, thinly sliced	1–4	2–8	3–10
salt	1 Tbsp	2 Tbsp	3 Tbsp
fresh, frozen, or dried unsweetened grated coconut	½ cup	1 cup	1½ cups
lemon juice	1 lemon	2 lemons	2½ lemons
chopped fresh cilantro, for garnish	2 Tbsp	¼ cup	⅔ cup

1. Soak the *chana* in ample boiled, hot water for at least 1 hour or in room temperature water for 6 hours to overnight. Drain and discard the water.

2. Place the inner pot in your Instant Pot and add the *chana* and cooking water. Lock the lid into place and make sure the pressure release valve is set to the sealing position (upwards). Press the **PRESSURE COOK** button and then press the **PRESSURE LEVEL** button until the panel reads **HIGH**. Adjust the cook time to 35 minutes.

3. On the stovetop, heat a shallow pan over medium-high heat. Add the *urad* and *chana* dals, red chiles, and coriander. Roast for 2 minutes, shaking the pan, until all the ingredients turn slightly brown and toasted. Transfer to a plate to cool for 5 minutes, then grind to a powder in a coffee grinder reserved for spices or with a mortar and pestle.

4. In the same pan, add the oil. Once the oil is hot, add the *hing* and mustard seeds. Cook for 2 minutes until the seeds start to pop and turn grey. *Keep a lid handy in case the mustard seeds splatter.*

5. Add the curry leaves and fresh chiles. Stir and cook for 1 minute until the leaves curl. Set aside.

6. Once the *chana* has finished cooking, release the pressure naturally for 10 minutes. Then manually release the remaining pressure, press **CANCEL**, and remove the lid. Add the powdered blend from Step 3, the salt, the oil mixture from Step 4, the coconut, the lemon juice, and the cilantro. Stir until the chickpeas are evenly coated. Serve this dish hot or cold as a snack or appetizer. *All the spices are edible, including the curry leaves.*

NOTE: The best kind of coconut to use is frozen grated coconut, found in most Indian grocery stores and some mainstream grocers. If you can't find fresh, use dried unsweetened coconut.

TRY THIS! Add some grated green mango or papaya (½ cup for a 3-quart IP or 1 cup for a 6-quart or 8-quart IP) along with the coconut.

Goan Black-Eyed Peas

This has become one of my family's favorite dishes. A specialty of Goan cuisine, it's made memorable by the flavor combination of black-eyed peas, coconut milk, spices, and a hint of brown sugar. The taste is irresistible and fuses together beautifully in the pressure cooker—the texture is almost silky.

	3 QUART	6 QUART	8 QUART
Yield	7 cups	14 cups	21 cups
Warm up	16 mins	27 mins	29 mins
Cook	30 mins	30 mins	30 mins
Cool down	10 mins NR + MR	10 mins NR + MR	10 mins NR + MR
Total time	soak + 56 mins	soak + 67 mins	soak + 69 mins

Ingredients	3 QUART	6 QUART	8 QUART
whole, dried black-eyed peas, picked over and washed	2 cups	4 cups	6 cups
oil or *ghee*	1 Tbsp	2 Tbsp	3 Tbsp
turmeric powder	½ tsp	1 tsp	1½ tsp
yellow onions, minced	1 small	1 medium	2 medium
piece of ginger, minced	1 (1-inch)	1 (2-inch)	1 (3-inch)
cloves of garlic, minced	2	4	6
fresh Thai or serrano chiles, stems removed, thinly sliced	1–3	2–6	3–8
tomatoes, puréed	1 medium	2 medium	3 medium
ground cumin	1 tsp	2 tsp	1 Tbsp
red chile powder or cayenne pepper	1 Tbsp	2 Tbsp	3 Tbsp
ground coriander	1 Tbsp	2 Tbsp	3 Tbsp
salt	1 Tbsp	2 Tbsp	3 Tbsp
light brown sugar	1 Tbsp	2 Tbsp	3 Tbsp
tamarind purée	1 Tbsp	2 Tbsp	3 Tbsp
water, for cooking	3 cups	6 cups	8 cups
coconut milk	1 cup	2 cups	3 cups
lemon juice	2 Tbsp	¼ cup	⅓ cup
chopped fresh cilantro, for garnish	1 Tbsp	2 Tbsp	¼ cup

1. Soak the black-eyed peas in ample boiled, hot water for 1 hour or in room temperature water for 6 hours to overnight. Drain and discard the water.

2. Place the inner pot in your Instant Pot. Select the **SAUTE** setting and adjust to **MORE**. When the indicator flashes **HOT**, add the oil. Once the oil is hot, add the turmeric and onions. Stir and cook for 2 minutes.

3. Add the ginger, garlic, and fresh chiles. Stir and cook for 1 minute.

4. Add the tomatoes. Stir and cook for 2 minutes, scraping the bottom of the pot to loosen anything stuck.

5. Press **CANCEL**. Add the cumin, red chile powder, coriander, salt, brown sugar, tamarind, black-eyed peas, and cooking water. Stir.

6. Lock the lid into place and make sure the pressure release valve is set to the sealing position (upwards). Press the **PRESSURE COOK** button and then press the **PRESSURE LEVEL** button until the panel reads **HIGH**. Adjust the cook time to 30 minutes.

7. Once the cooking is complete, release the pressure naturally for 10 minutes. Then manually release the remaining pressure, press **CANCEL**, and remove the lid. Add the coconut milk and lemon juice and stir. Cover the pot loosely with the lid and let the dish sit for 2 minutes. Garnish with the cilantro and serve with plain rice or crusty bread. *All the spices are edible.*

Chickpea Curry with Fresh Dill

This dish can be made with white chickpeas or with split and skinned black chickpeas called *chana dal*. It's a nice alternative to all the other heavily spiced and aromatic dishes that normally make up the North Indian diet. Try other herbs as well, including basil, cilantro, and mint for countless variations of this recipe.

	3 QUART	6 QUART	8 QUART
Yield	6 cups	12 cups	16 cups
Warm up	18 mins	26 mins	30 mins
Cook	40 mins	40 mins	40 mins
Cool down	10 mins NR + MR	10 mins NR + MR	10 mins NR + MR
Total time	soak + 68 mins	soak + 76 mins	soak + 80 mins

Ingredients	3 QUART	6 QUART	8 QUART
kabuli chana (dried white chickpeas), picked over and washed	2 cups	4 cups	6 cups
oil or *ghee*	1 Tbsp	2 Tbsp	3 Tbsp
hing (asafoetida) (optional)	1 pinch	2 pinches	3 pinches
turmeric powder	1 tsp	2 tsp	2½ tsp
yellow or red onions, minced	1 small	1 medium	2 medium
piece of ginger, minced	1 (1-inch)	1 (2-inch)	1 (3-inch)
cloves of garlic, minced	2	4	6
fresh Thai or serrano chiles, stems removed, thinly sliced	½–1	1–2	2–3
ground cumin	1 Tbsp	2 Tbsp	3 Tbsp
ground coriander	1 Tbsp	2 Tbsp	3 Tbsp
red chile powder or cayenne pepper	1 tsp	2 tsp	1 Tbsp
salt	2 tsp	1 Tbsp + 1 tsp	2 Tbsp
water, for cooking	3 cups	6 cups	8 cups
chopped fresh dill	½ cup	1 cup	1½ cups

1. Soak the *chana* in ample boiled, hot water for at least 1 hour or in room temperature water for 6 hours to overnight. Drain and discard the water.

2. Place the inner pot in your Instant Pot. Select the **SAUTE** setting and adjust to **MORE**. When the indicator flashes **HOT**, add the oil. Once the oil is hot, add the *hing* and turmeric. Stir and cook for 40 seconds.

3. Add the onions. Stir and cook for 3 minutes.

4. Add the ginger, garlic, and fresh chiles. Stir and cook for 2 minutes.

5. Press **CANCEL**. Add the cumin, coriander, red chile powder, salt, *chana*, and cooking water. Stir.

6. Lock the lid into place and make sure the pressure release valve is set to the sealing position (upwards). Press the **PRESSURE COOK** button and then press the **PRESSURE LEVEL** button until the panel reads **HIGH**. Adjust the cook time to 40 minutes.

7. Once the cooking is complete, release the pressure naturally for 10 minutes. Then manually release the remaining pressure, press **CANCEL**, and remove the lid. Add the dill and cover the pot loosely with the lid for 2 minutes until the dill wilts. Stir and serve over basmati rice or with Indian bread like *roti* or *naan*. *Feel free to substitute any combination of herbs. All the spices are edible.*

Dhania Waale Lobia

Cilantro-Infused Black-Eyed Peas

There is something oddly comforting about this tomato-based curry as the backdrop for black-eyed peas. While a simple recipe, this dish eaten over plain basmati rice truly shines. It's perfect on cold and snowy days, which we see more than our share of in Chicago.

	3 QUART	6 QUART	8 QUART
Yield	7 cups	15 cups	20 cups
Warm up	16 mins	34 mins	29 mins
Cook	30 mins	30 mins	30 mins
Cool down	10 mins NR + MR	10 mins NR + MR	10 mins NR + MR
Total time	soak + 56 mins	soak + 74 mins	soak + 69 mins

Ingredients	3 QUART	6 QUART	8 QUART
lobia (whole, dried black-eyed peas), picked over and washed	2 cups	4 cups	6 cups
oil or ghee	1 Tbsp	2 Tbsp	3 Tbsp
hing (asafoetida)	1 pinch	2 pinches	3 pinches
turmeric powder	½ tsp	1 tsp	1½ tsp
cinnamon stick	1 (1-inch)	1 (2-inch)	1 (3-inch)
whole cloves	3	6	8
yellow onions, minced	1 small	1 medium	2 medium
piece of ginger, puréed	1 (1-inch)	1 (2-inch)	1 (3-inch)
cloves of garlic, puréed	3	6	8
fresh Thai or serrano chiles, stems removed, thinly sliced	1–4	2–8	3–9
tomatoes, puréed	1 medium	2 medium	3 medium
unsalted tomato paste	1 Tbsp	2 Tbsp	3 Tbsp
kasoori methi (dried fenugreek leaves), lightly hand crushed to release flavor	2 Tbsp	¼ cup	½ cup
ground cumin	1 Tbsp	2 Tbsp	3 Tbsp
ground coriander	1 Tbsp	2 Tbsp	3 Tbsp
red chile powder or cayenne pepper	1 Tbsp	2 Tbsp	3 Tbsp
salt	1 Tbsp	2 Tbsp	3 Tbsp
minced fresh cilantro	1 cup	2 cups	2½ cups
water, for cooking	4 cups	8 cups	9 cups

1. Soak the *lobia* in ample boiled, hot water for at least 1 hour or in room temperature water for 6 hours to overnight. Drain and discard the water. Set aside.

2. Place the inner pot in your Instant Pot. Select the **SAUTE** setting and adjust to **MORE**. When the indicator flashes **HOT**, add the oil. Once the oil is hot, add the *hing*, turmeric, cinnamon, and cloves. Stir and cook for 40 seconds. *Because the oil pools to the sides, push the spices into the oil along the border of the inner pot so they can cook fully.*

3. Add the onions. Stir and cook for 3 minutes.

4. Add the ginger, garlic, and fresh chiles. Stir and cook for 1 minute.

5. Add the tomatoes and tomato paste. Stir and cook for 2 minutes, scraping the bottom to loosen anything stuck.

6. Press **CANCEL**. Add the *kasoori methi*, cumin, coriander, red chile powder, salt, *lobia*, cilantro, and cooking water. Stir.

7. Lock the lid into place and make sure the pressure release valve is set to the sealing position (upwards). Press the **PRESSURE COOK** button and then press the **PRESSURE LEVEL** button until the panel reads **HIGH**. Adjust the cook time to 30 minutes.

8. Once the cooking is complete, release the pressure naturally for 10 minutes. Then manually release the remaining pressure, press **CANCEL**, and remove the lid. Remove and discard the cinnamon stick and cloves or leave them in for flavor and eat around them. *All the other spices are edible.* Serve with basmati rice or Indian bread like *roti* or *naan*.

3 INSTANT POT–COOKED LEGUMES TO STOVETOP

When most people want to use whole beans, peas, or lentils (legumes) in a recipe, they usually reach for canned or frozen varieties. Even to someone who has grown up feasting on legumes, it can be intimidating to cook them from dried. You need to soak them first (or do you?), then cook them (how long?), and then if you are lucky, they are done. But what were you planning on cooking again? It's enough to make my head spin.

Now, I just reach for my Instant Pot. With a little planning, making wholesome, healthy, and salt-free legumes can be a cinch, helping you to avoid more expensive canned and frozen options. Not to mention, those cans won't take up storage space and you won't have to carry them from the grocery store. And, if you care about the environment—less garbage and waste! It's a win across the board.

I'd also argue that you get a better, more nutritious product. Cooked legumes from dried are tastier, absorb more flavor when cooked, and cook to a better texture than canned, which are often mushy. One reason folks think they don't like beans is because they've usually only had them from a can. I have a friend who thought chickpeas were made in cans—she'd never thought they were grown and then canned!

Though they can be made on the stovetop, this process is also cumbersome. It requires vigilance—you must keep an eye on the pot to make sure the water does not overflow and that the beans cook through. Time is something that as a busy mom of two with my own business I often do not have. With the Instant Pot, you avoid all the extra hassles and instead always end up with easy cooked beans, lentils, and peas on hand to sprinkle into salads, add to soups, whip up into hummus, or make into delicious Indian meals in minutes.

In this section, I have tested most of the popular legumes and given you exact soak times and water measurements to make them so that you have legumes that are perfectly cooked. Use the first set of recipes as your go-to whenever you plan to serve beans or lentils. Each of these recipes is for dried varieties cooked in water only. You'll end up with plain, cooked beans or lentils.

Then, go to the recipes that follow. There you'll find more than a dozen different and fun ways to prep 2 to 4 cups of your cooked beans and lentils. Feel free to swap out any legume for any preparation style. You'll have a blast experimenting with all the possibilities.

The beauty of it? Nothing ever goes to waste. I make large batches of beans and lentils and store them in 1–2 cup portions in baggies in the freezer. This way, whenever I need black beans for a Mexican dinner, I pull a bag out in the morning, so it's defrosted and ready for me in the evening. Legumes freeze extremely well, and this one step can change your reliance on take-out or the scramble to get a healthy meal on the table for your family. I often also store cooked masoor lentils, chickpeas, and kidney beans in glass jars in the fridge to top off my salads during the week. Just that little extra fiber and protein makes all the difference in feeling fuller and eating healthier.

Not even the cooking water needs to be wasted. While the water you soak dried beans in should always be discarded, the water you cook them in (if there is any after cooking) is filled with protein. It is called aquafaba and can be whipped up like egg whites, made into vegan mayo, and added to hummus for a fluffier texture instead of extra oil. The most useful kind is the water from cooked white chickpeas. I reserve liquids from darker beans for soups, some pastas, and hummus where the color blends. I store it in glass jars in my fridge or in ice-cube trays in my freezer. The amount of liquid after cooking varies depending on the legume.

Enjoy this section. I promise it's one that you'll come back to repeatedly!

RECITES

Sookha Kala Chana

Cooked, Plain Black Chickpeas

	3 QUART	6 QUART	8 QUART
Yield	4½ cups	10 cups	15½ cups
Warm up	12 mins	18 mins	23 mins
Cook	25 mins	25 mins	25 mins
Cool down	10 mins NR + MR	10 mins NR + MR	10 mins NR + MR
Total time	soak + 47 mins	soak + 53 mins	soak + 58 mins

Ingredients	3 QUART	6 QUART	8 QUART
kala chana (dried whole black chickpeas), picked over and washed	2 cups	4 cups	6 cups
water, for cooking	2 cups	4 cups	6 cups

1. Soak the *chana* in ample boiled, hot water for at least 1 hour or in room temperature water for 6 hours to overnight. Drain and discard the water.

2. Place the inner pot in your Instant Pot. Add the *chana* and cooking water. Lock the lid into place and make sure the pressure release valve is set to the sealing position (upwards). Press the **PRESSURE COOK** button and then press the **PRESSURE LEVEL** button until the panel reads **HIGH**. Adjust the cook time to 25 minutes.

3. Once the cooking is complete, release the pressure manually, press **CANCEL**, and remove the lid. *Cover the release valve loosely with a dishcloth you don't mind staining to avoid splattering.* Remove the *chana* with a slotted spoon, draining away any excess liquid. *You can also keep the liquid to eat with the* chana. If separating them, discard the liquid or keep it to add to other curries or soups. Store the cooked *chana* in the refrigerator for up to 1 week or in the freezer for up to 3 months portioned out in 1- to 2-cup servings for quicker use.

Sookha Kabuli Chana

Cooked, Plain White Chickpeas

	3 QUART	6 QUART	8 QUART
Yield	4½ cups	9 cups	14 cups
Warm up	12 mins	17 mins	22 mins
Cook	25 mins	25 mins	25 mins
Cool down	10 mins NR + MR	10 mins NR + MR	10 mins NR + MR
Total time	soak + 47 mins	soak + 52 mins	soak + 57 mins

Ingredients	3 QUART	6 QUART	8 QUART
kabuli chana (dried whole white chickpeas), picked over and washed	2 cups	4 cups	6 cups
water, for cooking	2 cups	4 cups	6 cups

1. Soak the *chana* in ample boiled, hot water for at least 1 hour or in room temperature water for 6 hours to overnight. Drain and discard the water.

2. Place the inner pot in your Instant Pot. Add the *chana* and cooking water. Lock the lid into place and make sure the pressure release valve is set to the sealing position (upwards). Press the **PRESSURE COOK** button and then press the **PRESSURE LEVEL** button until the panel reads **HIGH**. Adjust the cook time to 25 minutes.

3. Once the cooking is complete, release the pressure manually, press **CANCEL**, and remove the lid. *Cover the release valve loosely with a dishcloth you don't mind staining to avoid splattering.* Remove the *chana* with a slotted spoon, draining away any excess liquid. *You can also keep the liquid to eat with the* chana. If separating them, discard the liquid or keep it to add to other curries or soups. Store the cooked *chana* in the refrigerator for up to 1 week or in the freezer for up to 3 months portioned out in 1- to 2-cup servings for quicker use.

Sookha Sabut Masoor Dal

Cooked, Plain Brown Lentils

	3 QUART	6 QUART	8 QUART
Yield	5 cups	9 cups	14 cups
Warm up	13 mins	16 mins	21 mins
Cook	5 mins	5 mins	5 mins
Cool down	MR	MR	MR
Total time	soak + 18 mins	soak + 21 mins	soak + 26 mins

Ingredients	3 QUART	6 QUART	8 QUART
sabut masoor dal (whole, dried brown lentils), picked over and washed	2 cups	4 cups	6 cups
water, for cooking	2 cups	4 cups	6 cups

1. Soak the *masoor dal* in ample boiled, hot water for 10 minutes or in room temperature water for 20 minutes. Drain and discard the water. *If you soak it any longer, it will get mushy when cooking.*

2. Place the inner pot in your Instant Pot. Add the *dal* and the cooking water. Lock the lid into place and make sure the pressure release valve is set to the sealing position (upwards). Press the **PRESSURE COOK** button and then press the **PRESSURE LEVEL** button until the panel reads **HIGH**. Adjust the cook time to 5 minutes.

3. Once the cooking is complete, release the pressure manually, press **CANCEL**, and remove the lid. *Cover the release valve loosely with a dishcloth you don't mind staining to avoid splattering.* Remove the *dal* with a slotted spoon, draining away any excess liquid. *You can also keep the liquid to eat with the* dal. If separating them, discard the liquid or keep it to add to other curries or soups. Store the cooked *dal* in the refrigerator for up to 1 week or in the freezer up to 3 months portioned out in 1- to 2-cup servings for quick use.

Cooked, Plain Black Beans

	3 QUART	6 QUART	8 QUART
Yield	5 cups	9 cups	14 cups
Warm up	13 mins	16 mins	21 mins
Cook	15 mins	15 mins	15 mins
Cool down	10 mins NR + MR	10 mins NR + MR	10 mins NR + MR
Total time	soak + 38 mins	soak + 41 mins	soak + 46 mins

Ingredients	3 QUART	6 QUART	8 QUART
whole, dried black beans, picked over and washed	2 cups	4 cups	6 cups
water, for cooking	2 cups	4 cups	6 cups

1. Soak the black beans in ample boiled, hot water for at least 1 hour or in room temperature water for 6 hours to overnight. Drain and discard the water.

2. Place the inner pot in your Instant Pot. Add the beans and the cooking water. Lock the lid into place and make sure the pressure release valve is set to the sealing position (upwards). Press the **PRESSURE COOK** button and then press the **PRESSURE LEVEL** button until the panel reads **HIGH**. Adjust the cook time to 15 minutes.

3. Once the cooking is complete, release the pressure naturally for 10 minutes. Then manually release the remaining pressure, press **CANCEL**, and remove the lid. *Cover the release valve loosely with a dishcloth you don't mind staining to avoid splattering.* Remove the beans with a slotted spoon, draining away any excess liquid. *You can also keep the liquid to eat with the beans.* If separating, discard the liquid or keep it to add to other curries or soups. Store the cooked beans in the refrigerator for up to 1 week or in the freezer up to 3 months portioned out in 1- to 2-cup servings for quick use.

Sookha Lobia

Cooked, Plain Black-Eyed Peas

	3 QUART	6 QUART	8 QUART
Yield	5 cups	9 cups	14 cups
Warm up	12 mins	16 mins	21 mins
Cook	12 mins	12 mins	12 mins
Cool down	MR	MR	MR
Total time	soak + 24 mins	soak + 28 mins	soak + 33 mins

Ingredients	3 QUART	6 QUART	8 QUART
lobia (whole, dried black-eyed peas), picked over and washed	2 cups	4 cups	6 cups
water, for cooking	2½ cups	4½ cups	6½ cups

1. Soak the *lobia* in ample boiled, hot water for 10 minutes or in room temperature water for 20 minutes. Drain and discard the water.

2. Place the inner pot in your Instant Pot. Add the *lobia* and the cooking water. Lock the lid into place and make sure the pressure release valve is set to the sealing position (upwards). Press the **PRESSURE COOK** button and then press the **PRESSURE LEVEL** button until the panel reads **HIGH**. Adjust the cook time to 12 minutes.

3. Once the cooking is complete, release the pressure manually, press **CANCEL**, and remove the lid. Drain any excess liquid. *You can also keep the liquid to eat with the* lobia. If separating them, discard the liquid or keep it to add to other curries or soups. Store the cooked *lobia* in the refrigerator for up to 1 week or in the freezer up to 3 months portioned out in 1- to 2-cup servings for quick use.

Sookha Rajmah

Cooked, Plain Kidney Beans

	3 QUART	6 QUART	8 QUART
Yield	4½ cups	10 cups	15½ cups
Warm up	11 mins	18 mins	23 mins
Cook	25 mins	25 mins	25 mins
Cool down	MR	MR	MR
Total time	soak + 36 mins	soak + 43 mins	soak + 48 mins

Ingredients	3 QUART	6 QUART	8 QUART
rajmah (dried red kidney beans), picked over and washed	2 cups	4 cups	6 cups
water, for cooking	2 cups	4 cups	6 cups

1. Soak the *rajmah* in ample boiled, hot water for 30 minutes or in room temperature water for 1 hour. Drain and discard the water.

2. Place the inner pot in your Instant Pot. Add the *rajmah* and the cooking water. Lock the lid into place and make sure the pressure release valve is set to the sealing position (upwards). Press the **PRESSURE COOK** button and then press the **PRESSURE LEVEL** button until the panel reads **HIGH**. Adjust the cook time to 25 minutes.

3. Once the cooking is complete, release the pressure manually, press **CANCEL**, and remove the lid. Drain and discard any excess liquid. Store the cooked *rajmah* in the refrigerator for up to 1 week or in the freezer up to 3 months portioned out in 1- to 2-cup servings for quick use.

Sookha Sabut Moong Dal

Cooked, Plain Green *Moong*

	3 QUART	6 QUART	8 QUART
Yield	4½ cups	10 cups	15½ cups
Warm up	13 mins	19 mins	23 mins
Cook	15 mins	15 mins	15 mins
Cool down	MR	MR	MR
Total time	soak + 28 mins	soak + 34 mins	soak + 38 mins

Ingredients	3 QUART	6 QUART	8 QUART
sabut moong dal (whole, dried green *dal* with skin), picked over and washed	2 cups	4 cups	6 cups
water, for cooking	2 cups	4 cups	6 cups

1. Soak the *moong* in ample boiled, hot water for 10 minutes or in room temperature water for 20 minutes. Drain and discard the water.

2. Place the inner pot in your Instant Pot. Add the *moong* and cooking water. Lock the lid into place and make sure the pressure release valve is set to the sealing position (upwards). Press the **PRESSURE COOK** button and then press the **PRESSURE LEVEL** button until the panel reads **HIGH**. Adjust the cook time to 15 minutes.

3. Once the cooking is complete, release the pressure manually, press **CANCEL**, and remove the lid. *Cover the release valve loosely with a dishcloth you don't mind staining to avoid splattering.* Remove the *moong* with a slotted spoon, draining away any excess liquid. *You can also keep the liquid to eat with the* moong—*though there isn't usually much.* If separating them, discard the liquid or keep it to add to other curries or soups. Store the cooked *moong* in the refrigerator for up to 1 week or in the freezer for up to 3 months portioned out in 1- to 2-cup servings for quicker use.

Cooked, Plain Adzuki Beans

	3 QUART	6 QUART	8 QUART
Yield	5 cups	10 cups	15 cups
Warm up	13 mins	19 mins	23 mins
Cook	23 mins	23 mins	23 mins
Cool down	MR	MR	MR
Total time	soak + 36 mins	soak + 42 mins	soak + 46 mins

Ingredients	3 QUART	6 QUART	8 QUART
whole, dried adzuki beans, picked over and washed	2 cups	4 cups	6 cups
water, for cooking	2 cups	4 cups	6 cups

1. Soak the adzuki beans in ample boiled, hot water for 30 minutes or in room temperature water for 1 hour. Drain and discard the water.

2. Place the inner pot in your Instant Pot. Add the beans and cooking water. Lock the lid into place and make sure the pressure release valve is set to the sealing position (upwards). Press the **PRESSURE COOK** button and then press the **PRESSURE LEVEL** button until the panel reads **HIGH**. Adjust the cook time to 23 minutes.

3. Once the cooking is complete, release the pressure manually, press **CANCEL**, and remove the lid. *Cover the release valve loosely with a dishcloth you don't mind staining to avoid splattering.* Remove the beans with a slotted spoon, draining away any excess liquid. *You can also keep the liquid to eat with the beans.* If separating them, discard the liquid or keep it to add to other curries or soups. Store the cooked beans in the refrigerator for up to 1 week or in the freezer for up to 3 months portioned out in 1- to 2-cup servings for quicker use.

North Indian Hummus

YIELD: **2 CUPS**

2 cups cooked whole beans, lentils, or peas

Juice of 1 medium lemon

1 clove garlic, coarsely chopped

1 teaspoon coarse sea salt

1 teaspoon ground black pepper

½ teaspoon roasted cumin, ground (see recipe on page 23)

½ teaspoon ground coriander

¼ cup chopped fresh cilantro

⅓ cup plus 1 tablespoon olive oil

1–4 tablespoons water

½ teaspoon paprika (unsmoked), for garnish

1. In a food processor, combine the beans, lentils, or peas, lemon juice, garlic, salt, black pepper, cumin, coriander, and cilantro. Process until well mixed.

2. With the machine still running, add the oil. Continue to process until the mixture is creamy and smooth, adding water as needed, 1 tablespoon at a time.

3. Serve garnished with the paprika and with toasted *naan*, pita, or *papad* on the side.

TRY THIS! Garnish your dip with anything from chopped red onions to 1 teaspoon of grated fresh ginger, or even some finely sliced fresh chiles.

South Indian Hummus

YIELD: **2 CUPS**

2 cups cooked whole beans, lentils, or peas

Juice of 1 lemon

1 clove garlic, coarsely chopped

1 teaspoon coarse sea salt

1 teaspoon ground black pepper

½ teaspoon roasted cumin, ground (see recipe on page 23)

1 teaspoon *rasam* powder (see recipe on page 50) or *sambhar* powder (see recipe on page 71)

⅓ cup coconut oil

½ teaspoon *hing* (asafoetida)

1 teaspoon black mustard seeds

1–4 tablespoons water

½ teaspoon paprika (unsmoked), for garnish

1. In a food processor, combine the beans, lentils, or peas, lemon juice, garlic, salt, black pepper, cumin, and *rasam* powder or *sambhar* powder.

2. In a sauté pan, heat the oil over medium-high heat.

3. Add the *hing* and mustard. Cook until the seeds start to sizzle and pop, about 30 seconds. Be careful, you might need to cover the pan.

4. Add the oil mixture to the food processor and blend until creamy and smooth, adding water as needed, 1 tablespoon at a time. Serve garnished with the paprika and with toasted *naan*, pita, or *papad* on the side.

Indian-Inspired Soup

YIELD: **6 CUPS**

Soup is one of my easiest go-to meals on busy school nights. For my girls, it's a treat in a bowl; for me, it's fast and easy but nutritious as well. Cook your main ingredient (whole beans or lentils) ahead of time, and a fantastic soup will be at your fingertips any day of the week.

1 teaspoon vegetable oil

1 medium yellow onion, diced

3 medium carrots, peeled, trimmed, and diced or cut into thin rounds (1 heaping cup)

3 stalks celery, trimmed and diced (1 heaping cup)

4 cloves garlic, grated or minced

1 tablespoon *dhuli masoor dal* (dried, split, and skinned red lentils), picked over and washed

1½ teaspoons coarse sea salt

1 teaspoon ground cumin

½ teaspoon ground black pepper

6 cups water

2 cups cooked whole beans, lentils, or peas or a mixture

1. In a soup pot, heat the oil over medium-high heat.

2. Add the onion, carrots, celery, and garlic.

3. Cook for 1 to 2 minutes, until the vegetables soften and the onion browns slightly.

4. Add the *dal*, salt, cumin, pepper, and water and bring to a boil.

5. Reduce the heat and simmer uncovered for 20 minutes.

6. Add the cooked beans, lentils, or peas and heat through. Serve piping hot in bowls.

TRY THIS! Get creative with the veggies—spinach, red and/or green bell pepper, and broccoli all work.

Roasted *Masala* Beans or Lentils

YIELD: **4 CUPS**

This is how I get my kids to snack on chickpeas and other beans—by simply spicing and roasting them. This recipe is super easy, delicious, and healthy.

4 cups cooked whole beans, lentils, or peas

1 tablespoon *garam masala*, *chaat masala* (recipe follows), or *sambhar* powder (see recipe on page 71)

2 teaspoons coarse sea salt

2 tablespoons vegetable oil

1 teaspoon red chile powder, cayenne pepper, or paprika (unsmoked)

1. Set an oven rack at the highest position. Preheat oven to 425°F. Line a baking sheet with aluminum foil for easy cleanup.

2. In a large bowl, gently mix together the beans, lentils, or peas, *masala*, salt, and oil.

3. Arrange the seasoned beans, lentils, or peas in a single layer on the prepared baking sheet.

4. Bake for 15 minutes. Carefully take the tray out of the oven, mix gently so that the legumes cook evenly, and bake for another 10 minutes.

5. Cool for 15 minutes. Sprinkle with the red chile, cayenne, or paprika. Serve immediately as a salad, over brown or white basmati rice, or stuffed in a *roti* wrap.

CHAAT MASALA

YIELD: **2 CUPS**

½ heaping cup coriander seeds

2 heaping tablespoons cumin seeds

2 heaping tablespoons fennel seeds

8 whole dried red chiles, broken into pieces

½ cup whole black peppercorns

2 heaping teaspoons *amchur* (dried mango powder)

2 tablespoons *kala namak* (black salt)

2 heaping teaspoons ground ginger

2 heaping teaspoons *ajwain* (carom seeds)

1. In a shallow, heavy pan, dry roast the coriander, cumin, fennel, and red chiles over medium heat. Stay close, and shake the pan every 15 to 20 seconds to prevent the spices from burning. They should be just toasted and aromatic. After about 4 minutes of roasting, transfer the mixture to a plate and allow it to cool for 15 minutes.

2. Once the mixture is cool, transfer it to a spice grinder or the dry jug of a powerful blender, such as a Vitamix. Add the remaining ingredients and process to a fine powder. You may need to grind it—do so in small batches, depending on the size of your grinder. Sift after grinding to get a finer powder. Store in an airtight container for up to 6 months.

Cold North Indian Street Salad

Chaat | YIELD: **6 CUPS**

Indian salads are so easy to make and so much fun to eat. Fresh cilantro and spices, rather than oil, provide flavor, making these salads some of the healthiest around. You can use any cooked legumes, but one of my kids' favorites is brown whole lentils (*masoor dal*). Feel free to sub any veggies as well. I love grating in anything and everything, from beets, to carrots, to chopped cooked potatoes or even celery.

4 cups cooked whole beans, lentils, or peas

1 medium red onion, diced

1 medium tomato, diced

1 small cucumber, peeled and diced (½ cup)

1 medium daikon, peeled and grated (1 cup)

1–2 fresh Thai, serrano, or cayenne chiles, stems removed, chopped

¼ cup minced fresh cilantro

Juice of 1 large lemon

1 teaspoon coarse sea salt

½ teaspoon *kala namak* (black salt)

½ teaspoon *chaat masala* (see recipe on page 103)

½ teaspoon red chile powder or cayenne pepper

1 teaspoon fresh orange or white turmeric, peeled and grated (optional)

1. In a deep bowl, mix together all the ingredients. Serve immediately as a side salad or wrapped in a lettuce leaf, or do as I do, and serve with a side of warm brown basmati rice as a quick meal.

Warm North Indian Salad

YIELD: **3 CUPS**

This is a terrific and quick warm salad that is downright addictive. I really like it with cooked adzuki beans, but just about any legume would work. It's so versatile that you can serve it over a bed of lettuce, over rice, with Indian bread, or stuffed in a pita.

1 tablespoon vegetable oil

1 teaspoon cumin seeds

½ teaspoon turmeric powder

1 medium yellow or red onion, minced

1 (1-inch) piece ginger, peeled and sliced into matchsticks

2 cloves garlic, minced or grated

1–2 fresh Thai, serrano, or cayenne chiles, stems removed, chopped

2 cups cooked whole beans, lentils, or peas

1 teaspoon coarse sea salt

½ teaspoon red chile powder or cayenne pepper

½ teaspoon *kala namak* (black salt)

¼ cup chopped fresh cilantro

1. In a deep, heavy pan, heat the oil over medium-high heat.

2. Add the cumin and turmeric. Cook until the seeds sizzle, about 30 seconds.

3. Add the onion, ginger, garlic, and fresh chiles. Cook until browned, about 2 minutes.

4. Add the beans, lentils, or peas. Cook another 2 minutes.

5. Add the sea salt, chile powder, *kala namak*, and cilantro. Mix well and serve.

TRY THIS! I love mixing in freshly sprouted lentils or beans toward the end. You don't want to kill the nutritional properties of the sprouts by cooking them, but adding them at the end will give you just enough flavor. We love eating the sprout concoction as a breakfast with a side of toast.

Quickie *Masala* Beans or Lentils

YIELD: **5 CUPS**

1 cup *gila masala* (see recipe on page 159)

1 cup chopped vegetables (squash, pumpkin, bell peppers, carrots, corn, cauliflower, or spinach)

1–3 fresh Thai, serrano, or cayenne chiles, stems removed, chopped

1 teaspoon *garam masala*

1 teaspoon ground coriander

1 teaspoon roasted cumin, ground (see recipe on page 23)

½ teaspoon red chile powder or cayenne pepper

1½ teaspoons coarse sea salt

2 cups water

2 cups cooked whole beans, lentils, or peas

1 tablespoon chopped fresh cilantro, for garnish

1. In a deep, heavy saucepan, heat the *gila masala* over medium-high heat until it starts to bubble.

2. Add the vegetables, fresh chiles, *garam masala*, coriander, cumin, red chile powder, salt, and water. Cook until the vegetables soften, 15 to 20 minutes.

3. Add the beans, lentils, or peas. Cook until warmed through.

4. Garnish with the cilantro and serve immediately with brown or white basmati rice, *roti*, or *naan*.

South Indian Legume Salad with Coconut

YIELD: **4 CUPS**

2 tablespoons coconut oil

½ teaspoon *hing* (asafoetida)

1 teaspoon black mustard seeds

10–12 fresh curry leaves, coarsely chopped

2 tablespoons unsweetened shredded coconut

4 cups cooked whole beans, lentils, or peas

1 teaspoon coarse sea salt

1–2 fresh Thai, serrano, or cayenne chiles, stems removed, sliced lengthwise

1. In a deep, heavy pan, heat the oil over medium-high heat.

2. Add the *hing*, mustard, curry leaves, and coconut. Heat until the seeds pop, about 30 seconds. Be careful not to burn the curry leaves or coconut. The seeds can pop out, so keep a lid handy.

3. Add the beans, lentils, or peas, salt, and fresh chiles. Mix well and serve immediately.

NOTE: There is nothing better than freshly grated coconut, but if you cannot find it, use the dried grated variety from the grocery store. Just make sure it is unsweetened.

North Indian Curried Beans or Lentils

YIELD: **5 CUPS**

2 tablespoons vegetable oil

½ teaspoon *hing* (asafoetida)

2 teaspoons cumin seeds

½ teaspoon turmeric powder

1 (3-inch) cinnamon stick

1 cassia leaf or bay leaf

½ medium yellow or red onion, minced

1 (1-inch) piece ginger, peeled and grated or minced

4 cloves garlic, grated or minced

2 large tomatoes, peeled and diced

2–4 fresh Thai, serrano, or cayenne chiles, stems removed, chopped

4 cups cooked whole beans, lentils, or peas

4 cups water

1½ teaspoons coarse sea salt

1 teaspoon red chile powder or cayenne pepper

2 tablespoons chopped fresh cilantro, for garnish

1. In a heavy saucepan, heat the oil over medium-high heat.

2. Add the *hing*, cumin, turmeric, cinnamon, and cassia leaf and cook until the seeds sizzle, about 30 seconds.

3. Add the onion and cook until slightly browned, about 3 minutes. Stir frequently so the onion doesn't stick to the pan.

4. Add the ginger and garlic. Cook another 2 minutes.

5. Add the tomatoes and fresh chiles.

6. Reduce the heat to medium-low and cook for 3 to 5 minutes, until the tomatoes start to break down.

7. Add the beans, lentils, or peas and cook for another 2 minutes.

8. Add the water, salt, and red chile powder. Bring to a boil.

9. Once the mixture is boiling, reduce the heat and simmer for 10 to 15 minutes.

10. Garnish with the cilantro and serve with brown or white basmati rice, *roti*, or *naan*.

NOTE: This recipe calls for just the right amount of water. If the legumes absorb some of the liquid and you want more curry, just add a little more water, and add a little more salt to taste. You can remove the cassia or bay leaf or leave it in for flavor and eat around it.

Stovetop South Indian Beans or Lentils with Curry Leaves

YIELD: **6 CUPS**

This is one of my most popular recipes—people email me about it all the time. Who would have thought such simple ingredients (curry leaves, coconut milk, and *masoor dal*) could produce such magic? You can do the same with any legume. Just follow the recipe, and you'll have the essence of South Indian cuisine and ingredients right at your fingertips, literally in minutes.

2 tablespoons coconut oil

½ teaspoon *hing* (asafoetida)

½ teaspoon turmeric powder

1 teaspoon cumin seeds

1 teaspoon black mustard seeds

15–20 fresh curry leaves, coarsely chopped

6 whole dried red chiles, coarsely chopped

½ medium yellow or red onion, diced

1 (14-oz) can regular or light coconut milk

1 cup water

1 teaspoon *rasam* powder (see recipe on page 50) or *sambhar* powder (see recipe on page 71)

1½ teaspoons coarse sea salt

1 teaspoon red chile powder or cayenne pepper

3 cups cooked whole beans, lentils, or peas

1 tablespoon chopped fresh cilantro, for garnish

1. In a deep, heavy saucepan, heat the oil over medium-high heat.

2. Add the *hing*, turmeric, cumin, mustard, curry leaves, and dried chiles. Cook until the seeds sizzle, about 30 seconds. Mustard seeds can pop, so keep a lid handy.

3. Add the onion. Cook until browned, about 2 minutes, stirring frequently to prevent sticking.

4. Add the coconut milk, water, *rasam* powder or *sambhar* powder, salt, and red chile powder. Bring to a boil, and then reduce the heat and simmer for 1 to 2 minutes, until the flavors infuse the milk.

5. Add the beans, lentils, or peas. Warm through and simmer for 2 to 4 minutes, until the legumes are infused with flavor. Add another cup of water if you want a soupier consistency. Serve immediately, garnished with the cilantro, in deep bowls with brown or white basmati rice.

Goan-Inspired Curry with Coconut Milk

YIELD: **6 CUPS**

The tastes of Goa are influenced by the state's coastal location and its history as a Portuguese colony. Seafood and coconut milk are commonly woven through the cuisine in this region. This curry is a fun, light dish that is a nice diversion from some of the fiery curries of North India. Feel free to experiment with any beans, but chickpeas and black-eyed peas work best.

1 tablespoon vegetable oil

½ large onion, diced

1 (1-inch) piece ginger, peeled and grated or minced

4 cloves garlic, grated or minced

1 large tomato, diced

1–3 fresh Thai, serrano, or cayenne chiles, stems removed, chopped

1 tablespoon ground coriander

1 tablespoon ground cumin

1 teaspoon turmeric powder

1 teaspoon tamarind paste

1 heaping teaspoon *gur* (jaggery) or brown sugar

1½ teaspoons coarse sea salt

3 cups water

4 cups cooked whole beans, lentils, or peas (black-eyed peas are traditional)

1 cup regular or light coconut milk

Juice of ½ medium lemon

1 tablespoon chopped fresh cilantro, for garnish

1. In a deep, heavy saucepan, heat the oil over medium-high heat.

2. Add the onion and cook for 2 minutes, until slightly browned.

3. Add the ginger and garlic. Cook another minute.

4. Add the tomato, fresh chiles, coriander, cumin, turmeric, tamarind, jaggery, salt, and water.

5. Bring to a boil, reduce the heat, and simmer uncovered for 15 minutes.

6. Add the lentils, beans, or peas and coconut milk and heat through.

7. Add the lemon juice and garnish with the cilantro. Serve with brown or white basmati rice, *roti*, or *naan*.

Chana Masala Legumes

YIELD: **6 CUPS**

The spice *chana masala* is used to make the dish *chana masala.* I know, a little confusing. *Chana* refers to white chickpeas, but this recipe is in this section to inspire you to take your spice blend and use it for any beans, lentils, or peas. The tanginess of this *masala* comes from dried pomegranate seeds and mango powder. It's absolutely delicious and, I warn you, highly addictive once you see how easy it is to whip up.

2 tablespoons vegetable oil

1 heaping teaspoon cumin seeds

½ teaspoon turmeric powder

2 tablespoons *chana masala* (see recipe on page 81)

1 large yellow or red onion, diced

1 (2-inch) piece ginger, peeled and grated or minced

4 cloves garlic, minced

2 medium tomatoes, diced

1–3 fresh Thai, serrano, or cayenne chiles, stems removed, chopped

1 teaspoon red chile powder or cayenne pepper

1 tablespoon coarse sea salt

1 cup water

4 cups cooked whole beans, lentils, or peas (white chickpeas are traditional)

1. In a deep, heavy pan, heat the oil over medium-high heat.

2. Add the cumin, turmeric, and *chana masala* and cook until the seeds sizzle, about 30 seconds.

3. Add the onion and cook until soft, about a minute.

4. Add the ginger and garlic. Cook another minute.

5. Add the tomatoes, fresh chiles, red chile powder, salt, and water.

6. Bring to a boil, reduce the heat, and simmer the mixture for 10 minutes, until all the ingredients blend together.

7. Add the beans, lentils, or peas and cook through. Serve over brown or white basmati rice or with *roti* or *naan.*

Punjabi Curried Beans (*Rajmah*-Inspired Curry)

YIELD: **7 CUPS**

1 medium yellow or red onion, roughly chopped

1 (2-inch) piece ginger, peeled and roughly chopped

4 cloves garlic

2–4 fresh Thai, serrano, or cayenne chiles, stems removed, chopped

2 tablespoons vegetable oil

½ teaspoon *hing* (asafoetida)

2 teaspoons cumin seeds

1 teaspoon turmeric powder

1 (3-inch) cinnamon stick

2 whole cloves

1 black cardamom pod

2 medium tomatoes, peeled and diced

2 tablespoons unsalted tomato paste

4 cups cooked whole beans, lentils, or peas (kidney beans are traditional)

2 cups water

2 teaspoons coarse sea salt

2 teaspoons *garam masala*

1 teaspoon red chile powder or cayenne pepper

2 heaping tablespoons minced fresh cilantro

1. In a food processor, process the onion, ginger, garlic, and fresh chiles to a watery paste.

2. In a deep, heavy pan, heat the oil over medium-high heat.

3. Add the *hing*, cumin, turmeric, cinnamon, cloves, and cardamom. Cook until the mixture sizzles, about 30 seconds.

4. Slowly add the onion paste. Be careful—this can splatter when it hits the hot oil. Cook until browned, stirring occasionally, about 2 minutes.

5. Add the tomatoes, tomato paste, lentils, beans, or peas, water, salt, *garam masala*, and red chile powder.

6. Bring the mixture to a boil, then reduce the heat and simmer for 10 minutes.

7. Remove the whole spices. Add the cilantro and serve over a bed of brown or white basmati rice.

Stovetop *Sambhar*-Inspired Curry

YIELD: **9 CUPS**

2 cups cooked whole beans, lentils, or peas

9 cups water

1 medium potato (any kind), peeled and diced (about 2 cups)

1 teaspoon tamarind paste

5 cups vegetables (use a variety), diced and julienned

2 heaping tablespoons *sambhar* powder (see recipe on page 71)

1 tablespoon vegetable oil

1 teaspoon *hing* (asafoetida) (optional)

1 tablespoon black mustard seeds

5–8 whole dried red chiles, roughly chopped

8–10 fresh curry leaves, coarsely chopped

1 teaspoon red chile powder or cayenne pepper

1 tablespoon coarse sea salt

1. In a deep soup pot over medium-high heat, combine the beans, lentils, or peas, water, potato, tamarind, vegetables, and *sambhar* powder. Bring to a boil.

2. Reduce the heat and simmer for 15 minutes, until the vegetables wilt and soften.

3. Prepare the tempering (*tarka*). In a small pan, heat the oil over medium-high heat. Add the *hing* and mustard seeds. Mustard tends to pop, so keep a lid handy.

4. Once the seeds start to pop, quickly add the dried chiles and curry leaves. Cook for another 2 minutes, stirring frequently.

5. Once the curry leaves start to brown and curl up, add this mixture to the lentils. Cook for another 5 minutes.

6. Add the red chile powder and salt. Serve as a hearty soup, as a traditional side to *dosa*, or with brown or white basmati rice.

4

VEGETABLES

I like to say that in Indian cuisine vegetables shine. They take center stage and are downright addictive. There are many variations of these dishes, called *sabzi* (or *sabji*), which are typically drier than the recipes found in other chapters.

Because very little to no water is used to make them, this chapter was one of the most challenging to translate to an Instant Pot. A pressure cooker requires a certain amount of water to safely come to pressure.

I ended up using several key techniques including pulling out the inner pot to allow it to cool, removing the spice contents, and then pressure cooking the entire dish using a trivet to elevate the ingredients from the bottom of the pot. While the steps may take a little extra time and getting used to, I promise they are well worth the assurance that your Instant Pot operates safely while giving you a dish that honors its original consistency and taste profile.

Fiery Eggplant (page 133) >

RECIPES

Aloo Baingan

Spicy Punjabi Eggplant with Potatoes

Aloo Baingan is the first recipe I ever learned to cook. The key to success with this dish in the Instant Pot is to keep the eggplant pieces slightly larger, which cooks them through but also ensures they do not dissolve during cooking. I've made eggplant lovers out of many people who never thought it could taste this good.

	3 QUART	6 QUART	8 QUART
Yield	3 cups	7 cups	9 cups
Warm up	12 mins	13 mins	16 mins
Cook	3 mins	3 mins	3 mins
Cool down	MR	MR	MR
Total time	15 mins	16 mins	19 mins

Ingredients	3 QUART	6 QUART	8 QUART
oil or *ghee*	1 Tbsp	2 Tbsp	3 Tbsp
hing (asafoetida) (optional)	1 pinch	2 pinches	3 pinches
cumin seeds	2 tsp	1 Tbsp + 1 tsp	2 Tbsp
turmeric powder	½ tsp	1 tsp	1½ tsp
yellow or red onions, coarsely chopped	1 small	1 medium	2 medium
piece of ginger, cut into 1½-inch matchsticks	1 (1-inch)	1 (2-inch)	1 (3-inch)
cloves of garlic, minced	3	6	8
fresh Thai or serrano chiles, stems removed, thinly sliced	½–3	1–6	2–7
potatoes (russet or yellow), peeled and coarsely chopped	1 small	1 medium	2 medium
garam masala	2 tsp	1 Tbsp + 1 tsp	2 Tbsp
ground coriander	2 tsp	1 Tbsp + 1 tsp	2 Tbsp
red chile powder or cayenne pepper	2 tsp	1 Tbsp + 1 tsp	2 Tbsp
salt	2 tsp	1 Tbsp + 1 tsp	2 Tbsp
water	¼ cup	½ cup	¾ cup
eggplant, cut into 2-inch pieces	6 cups (1 medium)	12 cups (2 medium)	16 cups (3 medium)
tomatoes, coarsely chopped	1 medium	2 medium	3 medium
chopped fresh cilantro, for garnish	1 Tbsp	2 Tbsp	3 Tbsp

1. Place the inner pot in your Instant Pot. Select the **SAUTE** setting and adjust to **NORMAL**. When the indicator flashes **HOT**, add the oil. Once the oil is hot, add the *hing* and cumin. Stir and cook for 1 minute until the seeds turn reddish brown. *Because the oil pools to the sides, push the spices into the oil along the border so they cook fully.*

2. Add the turmeric. Stir and cook for 30 seconds.

3. Add the onions. Stir and cook for 2 minutes.

4. Add the ginger, garlic, and fresh chiles. Stir and cook for 1 minute.

5. Add the potatoes. Stir and cook for 1 minute.

6. Add the *garam masala*, coriander, red chile powder, and salt. Stir and cook for 30 seconds.

7. Press **CANCEL**. Carefully remove the inner pot and place it on a heat-resistant surface. Transfer the contents to a bowl, scraping the bottom.

8. Return the inner pot to the base. Add the water, scrape anything remaining in the pot loose, and then position a trivet in the pot. Add the eggplant, tomatoes, and mixture from Step 7 in that order. Do NOT stir.

9. Lock the lid into place. Make sure the pressure release valve is set to the sealing position (upwards). Press the **PRESSURE COOK** button and then press the **PRESSURE LEVEL** button until the panel reads **LOW**. Adjust the cook time to 3 minutes.

10. Once the cooking is complete, release the pressure manually, press **CANCEL**, and remove the lid. Remove the trivet with tongs and transfer the cooked dish immediately to an unheated container to limit the moisture released. Stir the contents until the eggplant is evenly coated and garnish with the cilantro. Eat with Indian bread like *roti* or *naan* or with rice. *All the spices are edible.*

Aloo Gobi

Spiced Cauliflower and Potato

	3 QUART	6 QUART	8 QUART
Yield	3 cups	6 cups	11 cups
Warm up	11 mins	16 mins	20 mins
Cook	2 mins	2 mins	2 mins
Cool down	MR	MR	MR
Total time	13 mins	18 mins	22 mins

In our home we eat this dish weekly. Because we have such a high bar for it, I was a little nervous about trying it in the Instant Pot. The first few batches were mushy. Eventually, I realized that to keep the cauliflower from dissolving, you need to keep the pieces slightly larger and reduce the cook time.

Ingredients	3 QUART	6 QUART	8 QUART
oil or *ghee*	1 Tbsp	2 Tbsp	3 Tbsp
hing (asafoetida) (optional)	1 pinch	2 pinches	3 pinches
cumin seeds	2 tsp	1 Tbsp + 1 tsp	2 Tbsp
turmeric powder	½ tsp	1 tsp	1½ tsp
yellow or red onions, coarsely chopped	1 small	1 medium	2 medium
piece of ginger, minced	1 (1-inch)	1 (2-inch)	1 (3-inch)
cloves of garlic, minced	3	6	8
fresh Thai or serrano chiles, stems removed, thinly sliced	½–3	1–6	2–8
potatoes (russet or yellow), peeled and coarsely chopped	1 small	1 medium	2 medium
water	¼ cup	½ cup	¾ cup
frozen peas, slightly defrosted	¼ cup	½ cup	¾ cup
garam masala	2 tsp	1 Tbsp + 1 tsp	2 Tbsp
ground coriander	2 tsp	1 Tbsp + 1 tsp	2 Tbsp
red chile powder or cayenne pepper	1 tsp	1 Tbsp + 1 tsp	2 Tbsp
salt	2 tsp	1 Tbsp + 1 tsp	2 Tbsp
cauliflower, cut into 2½-inch pieces	5 cups (1 medium head)	10 cups (2 medium heads)	16 cups (2½ medium heads)
chopped fresh cilantro, for garnish	1 Tbsp	2 Tbsp	3 Tbsp

1. Place the inner pot in your Instant Pot. Select the **SAUTE** setting and adjust to **NORMAL**. When the indicator flashes **HOT**, add the oil. Once the oil is hot, add the *hing* and cumin. Stir and cook for 1 minute until the seeds turn reddish brown. *Because the oil pools to the sides, push the spices into the oil along the border so they cook fully.*

2. Add the turmeric. Stir and cook for 30 seconds.

3. Add the onions. Stir and cook for 2 minutes.

4. Add the ginger, garlic, and fresh chiles. Stir and cook for 1 minute.

5. Add the potatoes. Stir and cook for 1 minute.

6. Press **CANCEL**. Carefully remove the inner pot and place it on a heat-resistant surface. Add the water, peas, *garam masala*, coriander, red chile powder, and salt. Stir, scraping the bottom to loosen anything stuck.

7. Add the cauliflower and return the inner pot to the base. Do NOT stir.

8. Lock the lid into place. Make sure the pressure release valve is set to the sealing position (upwards). Press the **PRESSURE COOK** button and then press the **PRESSURE LEVEL** button until the panel reads **LOW**. Adjust the cook time to 2 minutes.

9. Once the cooking is complete, release the pressure manually, press **CANCEL**, and remove the lid. Transfer the cooked dish immediately to an unheated container to limit the moisture released. Stir the contents until the cauliflower is evenly coated and garnish with the cilantro. Eat with Indian bread like *roti* or *naan*, serve with rice, or use as a stuffing for homemade Indian bread like *parantha*. *All the spices are edible.*

Band Gobi

Punjabi-Style Cabbage

It's hard to believe that simple cabbage can taste so good. There is just something about all these spices combined with the crunchiness and slight sweetness of white cabbage. When my kids were little, they would go crazy rolling it up in a roti and drizzling it with *raita*.

	3 QUART	6 QUART	8 QUART
Yield	4 cups	5 cups	10 cups
Warm up	9 mins	14 mins	14 mins
Cook	3 mins	3 mins	3 mins
Cool down	MR	MR	MR
Total time	12 mins	17 mins	17 mins

Ingredients	3 QUART	6 QUART	8 QUART
vegetable oil	1 Tbsp	2 Tbsp	3 Tbsp
hing (asafoetida) (optional)	1 pinch	2 pinches	3 pinches
cumin seeds	2 tsp	1 Tbsp + 1 tsp	1 Tbsp + 2 tsp
turmeric powder	½ tsp	1 tsp	1½ tsp
yellow or red onions, thinly sliced	1 small	1 medium	2 medium
piece of ginger, minced	1 (1-inch)	1 (2-inch)	1 (3-inch)
cloves of garlic, minced	3	6	8
fresh Thai or serrano chiles, stems removed, thinly sliced	½–3	1–6	2–7
potatoes (russet or yellow), peeled and coarsely chopped	1 small	1 medium	2 medium
frozen peas, slightly defrosted	¼ cup	½ cup	¾ cup
garam masala	1 tsp	2 tsp	1 Tbsp
ground coriander	1 tsp	2 tsp	1 Tbsp
ground black pepper	½ tsp	1 tsp	1½ tsp
red chile powder or cayenne pepper	½ tsp	1 tsp	1½ tsp
salt	2 tsp	1 Tbsp	1 Tbsp + 1 tsp
water	¼ cup	½ cup	¾ cup
white cabbage, finely shredded	5 cups (1 small head)	10 cups (1 medium head)	15 cups (1 large head)

1. Place the inner pot in your Instant Pot. Select the **SAUTE** setting and adjust to **NORMAL**. When the indicator flashes **HOT**, add the oil. Once the oil is hot, add the *hing* and cumin. Stir and cook for 40 seconds until the seeds turn reddish brown. *Because the oil pools to the sides, push the spices into the oil along the border so they cook fully.*

2. Add the turmeric. Stir and cook for 30 seconds.

3. Add the onions. Stir and cook for 1 minute.

4. Add the ginger, garlic, and fresh chiles. Stir and cook for 1 minute.

5. Add the potatoes. Stir and cook for 1 minute.

6. Add the peas, *garam masala*, coriander, black pepper, red chile powder, and salt. Stir and cook for 1 minute.

7. Press **CANCEL**. Carefully remove the inner pot and place it on a heat-resistant surface. Transfer the contents to a bowl.

8. Add the water to the inner pot and stir, scraping the bottom to loosen anything stuck.

9. Add the cabbage and the mixture from Step 7 in that order. Do NOT stir.

10. Return the inner pot to the base and lock the lid into place. Make sure the pressure release valve is set to the sealing position (upwards). Press the **PRESSURE COOK** button and then press the **PRESSURE LEVEL** button until the panel reads **LOW**. Adjust the cook time to 3 minutes.

11. Once the cooking is complete, release the pressure manually, press **CANCEL**, and remove the lid. Transfer the cooked dish immediately to an unheated container to limit the moisture released. Stir the contents until the cabbage is evenly coated. Eat with Indian bread like *roti* or *naan* or with rice. *All the spices are edible.*

Methi Gajar

Fenugreek Carrots

I'm not sure why I'm obsessed with a carrot dish, but this one is heavenly. There's something about the sweetness of this vegetable that blends perfectly with the slight bitterness of the fenugreek. The step of sautéing in the end is important in the Instant Pot to ensure that all the liquid dries up. It is delicious rolled up in a *roti*.

	3 QUART	6 QUART	8 QUART
Yield	3 cups	6 cups	8 cups
Warm up	8 mins	14 mins	15 mins
Cook	5 mins	5 mins	5 mins
Cool down	MR	MR	MR
Total time	13 mins + sauté	19 mins + sauté	20 mins + sauté

Ingredients	3 QUART	6 QUART	8 QUART
oil or *ghee*	1 Tbsp	2 Tbsp	3 Tbsp
hing (asafoetida) (optional)	1 pinch	2 pinches	3 pinches
turmeric powder	½ tsp	1 tsp	2 tsp
garam masala	2 tsp	1 Tbsp + 1 tsp	2 Tbsp
amchur (dried mango powder)	1 tsp	2 tsp	1 Tbsp
carrots, peeled and cut into ⅜-inch-thick rounds	4 cups (4 large)	8 cups (8 large)	12 cups (12 large)
salt	2 tsp	1 Tbsp + 1 tsp	2 Tbsp
water	¼ cup	½ cup	¾ cup
kasoori methi (dried fenugreek leaves), lightly hand crushed to release flavor	¼ cup	⅓ cup	½ cup

1. Place the inner pot in your Instant Pot. Select the **SAUTE** setting and adjust to **NORMAL**. When the indicator flashes **HOT**, add the oil. Once the oil is hot, add the *hing* and turmeric. Stir and cook for 40 seconds. *Because the oil pools to the sides, push the turmeric into the oil along the border so it can cook fully.*

2. Add the *garam masala* and *amchur*. Stir and cook for 30 seconds.

3. Press **CANCEL**. Carefully remove the inner pot and place it on a heat-resistant surface. Add the carrots, salt, and water. Stir.

4. Return the inner pot to the base and lock the lid into place. Make sure the pressure release valve is set to the sealing position (upwards). Press the **PRESSURE COOK** button and then press the **PRESSURE LEVEL** button until the panel reads **HIGH**. Adjust the cook time to 5 minutes.

5. Once the cooking is complete, release the pressure manually, press **CANCEL**, and remove the lid. Add the *kasoori methi* and stir. *If you find fresh methi, you can also add a cup of fresh leaves with the dried. Do not use fenugreek seeds, which cook differently.*

6. Press the **SAUTE** button and adjust to **MORE**. Simmer uncovered for about 5 minutes, until any moisture dries up. Serve immediately with a warm *roti* or *naan*. *All the spices are edible.*

NOTE: If the carrots are very fresh, I just scrub them down and don't bother peeling them.

Sambhar (page 70)

Paitha

Spicy Butternut Squash

	3 QUART	6 QUART	8 QUART
Yield	4 cups	8 cups	12 cups
Warm up	16 mins	30 mins	30 mins
Cook	3 mins	3 mins	3 mins
Cool down	MR	MR	MR
Total time	19 mins	33 mins	33 mins

The Punjabi take on squash is out of this world. It's a crazy mix of salty, spicy, and sweet, with a hint of tart. The first time I learned how to make this dish successfully was in Hawaii, with my fellow foodie—Mukta. My mom helped adapt it from stovetop to slow cooker. And now, I've perfected it in the Instant Pot.

Ingredients	3 QUART	6 QUART	8 QUART
oil or *ghee*	1 Tbsp	2 Tbsp	3 Tbsp
hing (asafoetida) (optional)	1 pinch	2 pinches	3 pinches
cumin seeds	1 tsp	2 tsp	1 Tbsp
turmeric powder	½ tsp	1 tsp	1½ tsp
black cardamom pods (optional)	1	2	2
cinnamon stick	1 (1-inch)	1 (2-inch)	1 (3-inch)
fenugreek seeds	½ tsp	1 tsp	1½ tsp
yellow onion, minced	½ small	1 small	1 medium
piece of ginger, minced	1 (1-inch)	1 (2-inch)	1 (3-inch)
fresh Thai or serrano chiles, stems removed, sliced lengthwise	½–3	1–6	2–7
garam masala	2 tsp	1 Tbsp + 1 tsp	2 Tbsp
ground coriander	2 tsp	1 Tbsp + 1 tsp	2 Tbsp
amchur (dried mango powder)	2 tsp	1 Tbsp + 1 tsp	2 Tbsp
red chile powder or cayenne pepper	2 tsp	1 Tbsp + 1 tsp	2 Tbsp
salt	1 Tbsp	2 Tbsp	3 Tbsp
light brown sugar	1 Tbsp	2 Tbsp	3 Tbsp
water, divided	¼ cup + 1 Tbsp	½ cup + 1 Tbsp	¾ cup + 1 Tbsp
peeled and diced butternut squash (1-inch cubes)	7 cups (4½ lbs)	14 cups (9 lbs)	20 cups (13 lbs)
lemon juice	½ lemon	1 lemon	1½ lemons
chopped fresh cilantro, for garnish	1 Tbsp	2 Tbsp	3 Tbsp

1. Place the inner pot in your Instant Pot. Select the **SAUTE** setting and adjust to **MORE**. When the indicator flashes **HOT**, add the oil. Once the oil is hot, add the *hing* and cumin. Stir and cook for 40 seconds until the seeds turn reddish brown. *Because the oil pools to the sides, push the spices into the oil along the border so they cook fully.*

2. Add the turmeric, cardamom, cinnamon, and fenugreek. Stir and cook for 30 seconds. *Do not overcook or the fenugreek will get bitter.*

3. Add the onion. Stir and cook for 1 minute.

4. Add the ginger and fresh chiles. Stir and cook for 1 minute.

5. Press **CANCEL**. Add the *garam masala*, coriander, *amchur*, red chile powder, salt, and brown sugar. Stir.

6. Carefully transfer the inner pot to a heat-resistant surface. Add 1 tablespoon of water to deglaze and scrape the bottom to loosen anything stuck. Transfer this mixture to a bowl.

7. Return the inner pot to the base. Pour in the water, place a trivet in the pot, and add the squash and the mixture from Step 6 in that order. Do NOT stir.

8. Lock the lid into place and make sure the pressure release valve is set to the sealing position (upwards). Press the **PRESSURE COOK** button and then press the **PRESSURE LEVEL** button until the panel reads **HIGH**. Adjust the cook time to 3 minutes.

9. Once the cooking is complete, release the pressure manually, press **CANCEL**, and remove the lid. Carefully move the inner pot to a heat-resistant surface and remove the trivet with tongs. Transfer the contents to an unheated container to limit the amount of moisture released. Remove and discard the cardamom and cinnamon or leave them in for flavor and eat around them. *All the other spices are edible.* Add the lemon juice and stir the contents gently until the squash is evenly coated and garnish with the cilantro. *The squash should remain in chunks.* Eat with Indian bread like *roti* or *naan*.

Palak Paneer

Curried Spinach with Paneer

This dish needs no introduction. Anyone who has ever had Indian food has tasted *palak paneer*. I'm here to tell you that it's a cinch to make in the Instant Pot. *Paneer* is best added after cooking and can be made at home on the stovetop using my recipe on page 128. You'll be a pro the first time you try it—it's truly that simple.

	3 QUART	6 QUART	8 QUART
Yield	2 cups before *paneer* + cream	4 cups before *paneer* + cream	7½ cups before *paneer* + cream
Warm up	7 mins	10 mins	12 mins
Cook	0 mins	0 mins	0 mins
Cool down	MR	MR	MR
Total time	7 mins + sauté	10 mins + sauté	12 mins + sauté

Ingredients	3 QUART	6 QUART	8 QUART
oil or *ghee*	1 Tbsp	2 Tbsp	3 Tbsp
hing (asafoetida) (optional)	1 pinch	2 pinches	3 pinches
cumin seeds	2 tsp	1 Tbsp	1 Tbsp + 2 tsp
turmeric powder	½ tsp	1 tsp	2 tsp
yellow or red onions, coarsely chopped	1 small	1 medium	2 medium
piece of ginger, cut into small pieces	1 (2-inch)	1 (3-inch)	1 (4-inch)
cloves of garlic, coarsely chopped	4	6	12
fresh Thai or serrano chiles, stems removed, thinly sliced	½–4	2–6	6–8
water	½ cup	1 cup	2 cups
fresh spinach, tightly packed, trimmed, and chopped	4 cups (4.2 oz)	10 cups (10.6 oz)	16 cups (1.1 lb)
kasoori methi (dried fenugreek leaves) (optional), gently crushed in one hand to release flavor	2 tsp	2 Tbsp	½ cup
cornmeal (optional)	2 tsp	2 Tbsp	¼ cup
tomato, coarsely chopped	1 small	1 medium	1 large
unsalted tomato paste	1 Tbsp	2 Tbsp	¼ cup
garam masala	2 tsp	1 Tbsp	2 Tbsp
ground coriander	2 tsp	1 Tbsp	2 Tbsp
red chile powder or cayenne pepper	2 tsp	1 Tbsp	2 Tbsp
salt	2 tsp	1 Tbsp	2 Tbsp
diced *paneer*	2 cups	4 cups	8 cups
heavy cream or half-and-half (dairy or alternative) (optional)	2 Tbsp	3 Tbsp	¼ cup

1. Place the inner pot in your Instant Pot. Select the **SAUTE** setting and adjust to **MORE**. When the indicator flashes **HOT**, add the oil. Once the oil is hot, add the *hing* and cumin. Stir and cook for 40 seconds until the seeds turn reddish brown. *Because the oil pools to the sides, push the spices into the oil along the border so they cook fully.*

2. Add the turmeric. Stir and cook for 30 seconds.

3. Add the onions. Stir and cook for 1 minute.

4. Add the ginger, garlic, and fresh chiles. Stir and cook for 1 minute.

5. Press **CANCEL**. Carefully remove the inner pot and place it on a heat-resistant surface. Add the water and stir, scraping loose anything stuck to the bottom. Let the pot cool for 5 minutes. *This prevents a BURN warning later.*

6. Return the inner pot to your Instant Pot and add the spinach, *kasoori methi*, cornmeal, tomato, tomato paste, *garam masala*, coriander, red chile powder, and salt in that order. Do NOT stir. *It's important to add the tomato and tomato paste on top of the spinach to avoid a BURN warning. Press down a bit if the contents go slightly above the maximum fill line.*

7. Lock the lid into place. Make sure that the pressure release valve is set to the sealing position (upwards). Press the **PRESSURE COOK** button and then press the **PRESSURE LEVEL** button until the panel reads **LOW**. Adjust the cook time to 0. *A zero cook time simply means the dish will cook sufficiently during the warm-up time, and that no additional time is needed.*

8. Once the cooking is complete, release the pressure manually, press **CANCEL**, and remove the lid. Use an immersion or regular blender to process until smooth or leave a little texture—your choice. *If using an immersion blender, you may need to tilt the pot so the contents don't splash.*

9. Press the **SAUTE** button and adjust to **MORE**. Immediately add the *paneer*. Cook for up to 3 minutes. You can loosely leave the lid on to avoid splashes. *Alternatively, pan or deep fry the paneer separately.* Add the cream if using and stir. Serve over basmati rice or with Indian bread like *roti* or *naan*. *All the spices are edible.*

PANEER

YIELD: **12 OUNCES**

8 cups milk (whole, low-fat, or skim)

½ cup fresh lemon juice, buttermilk, or plain, unsweetened yogurt

1. In a heavy medium saucepan, bring the milk to a boil over medium-high heat. Be careful not to let it boil too fast, as it could boil over. If you let it simmer over too low of a heat, it could collect and burn at the bottom of the pan. The boiling process should take just a few minutes.

2. Remove the pan from the heat and immediately add the lemon juice, buttermilk, or yogurt. Mix well and then cover the pan tightly. Let it sit for at least 10 minutes. Pour the mixture into a large colander lined with cheesecloth. Pull the cheesecloth together at the corners, tie the ends together, and hang the sack above your sink for a few hours. Alternatively, you can use a slotted spoon to scrape the cheese off the top of the pan. Put this cheese on a flat plate, put another plate on top (so the bottom touches the cheese), and put a heavy saucepan on top of that. Let it sit for at least 1 hour.

3. Cut the cheese into 1-inch cubes. Use as is, or fry until golden brown.

NOTES: Lemon, buttermilk, and yogurt all work equally well to make *paneer*, but they all impart a slightly different taste profile. Experiment and decide what you prefer. If the *paneer* does not set in the time suggested above, add more lemon, buttermilk, or yogurt 1 tablespoon at a time until it does.

If you prefer, you can substitute cubed, firm tofu either fresh, baked, or fried.

Paneer isn't complicated to make and is worth the effort, because when you make it yourself you can use organic and/or low-fat milk, if you prefer.

Sarson ka Saag

Punjabi Mustard Greens

This is a dish close to the hearts of most Punjabis. When making this in the Instant Pot, it's important to cook it slightly longer than you would just spinach. Mustard greens need to be cooked down quite a bit. This is also a little easier to navigate because you need water, which is perfect for a pressure cooker.

	3 QUART	6 QUART	8 QUART
Yield	3 cups	6 cups	8 cups
Warm up	9 mins	12 mins	14 mins
Cook	8 mins	8 mins	8 mins
Cool down	MR	MR	MR
Total time	17 mins + tarka	20 mins + tarka	22 mins + tarka

Ingredients (for IP)	3 QUART	6 QUART	8 QUART
water	1½ cups	3 cups	4 cups
mustard greens, washed, trimmed, and coarsely chopped	4 cups	8 cups	12 cups
spinach, washed, trimmed, and coarsely chopped	1 cup	2 cups	3 cups
kasoori methi (dried fenugreek leaves) (optional), lightly hand crushed to release flavor	¼ cup	½ cup	¾ cup
yellow or red onions, coarsely chopped	1 small	1 medium	2 medium
piece of ginger, cut into small pieces	1 (2-inch)	1 (4-inch)	1 (6-inch)
cloves of garlic, coarsely chopped	8	16	20
fresh Thai or serrano chiles, stems removed, coarsely chopped	1–4	2–8	3–10
turmeric powder	1 tsp	2 tsp	1 Tbsp
garam masala	1 Tbsp	2 Tbsp	3 Tbsp
ground coriander	1 Tbsp	2 Tbsp	3 Tbsp
red chile powder or cayenne pepper	1 Tbsp	2 Tbsp	3 Tbsp
salt	2 tsp	1 Tbsp + 1 tsp	2 Tbsp
cornmeal	2 tsp	1 Tbsp + 1 tsp	2 Tbsp

Ingredients (for *tarka*)	3 QUART	6 QUART	8 QUART
ghee or oil	1 Tbsp	2 Tbsp	3 Tbsp
hing (asafoetida) (optional)	1 pinch	2 pinches	3 pinches
yellow or red onions, finely minced	1 small	1 medium	2 medium
fresh Thai or serrano chiles, stems removed, thinly sliced	½–2	1–4	2–6

1. Place the inner pot in your Instant Pot. Add the water, mustard greens, spinach, *kasoori methi*, onions, ginger, garlic, fresh chiles, turmeric, *garam masala*, coriander, red chile powder, salt, and cornmeal in that order. Do NOT stir. *Mustard greens can be gritty and need to be washed several times ahead of cooking.*

2. Lock the lid into place. Make sure that the pressure release valve is set to the sealing position (upwards). Press the **PRESSURE COOK** button and then press the **PRESSURE LEVEL** button until the panel reads **HIGH**. Adjust the cook time to 8 minutes.

3. Once the cooking is complete, release the pressure manually, press **CANCEL**, and remove the lid. Stir and use an immersion or regular blender to process until smooth or leave a little texture—your choice. *If using an immersion blender, you may need to tilt the pot so the contents don't splash. I prefer my* saag *smooth.*

4. On the stovetop, prepare the *tarka* by heating a shallow pan over medium-high heat. Once hot, add the *ghee*. Once the *ghee* starts to melt, add the *hing*, onions, and fresh chiles. Cook until slightly brown, about 3 minutes. Add this immediately to the *saag*. Stir and serve with corn *rotis*, regular *rotis*, or naan.

TRY THIS! Pour the finished dish over a piece of freshly made corn bread or cooked polenta.

Rase Wale Aloo

Saucy Punjabi Potatoes

This recipe is a favorite weekend lunch item. When I was testing it for the Instant Pot, I was lucky enough to have my parents visit from Pennsylvania. My father suggested adding raisins—something they did in his village of Bhikhi when he was growing up in India. It was a brilliant addition, giving the dish a gourmet feel.

	3 QUART	6 QUART	8 QUART
Yield	8 cups	15 cups	19 cups
Warm up	19 mins	31 mins	32 mins
Cook	3 mins	3 mins	3 mins
Cool down	MR	MR	MR
Total time	22 mins	34 mins	35 mins

Ingredients	3 QUART	6 QUART	8 QUART
oil or *ghee*	1 Tbsp	2 Tbsp	3 Tbsp
hing (asafoetida) (optional)	1 pinch	2 pinches	3 pinches
cumin seeds	2 tsp	1 Tbsp	1 Tbsp + 2 tsp
turmeric powder	½ tsp	1 tsp	2 tsp
cinnamon stick	1 (1-inch)	1 (2-inch)	1 (3-inch)
black cardamom pods	1	2	3
cassia leaves (or bay leaves)	1 (or 2)	1 (or 3)	2 (or 4)
yellow or red onions, puréed	1 small	1 medium	2 medium
piece of ginger, puréed	1 (1-inch)	1 (2-inch)	1 (3-inch)
cloves of garlic, puréed	2	4	5
fresh Thai or serrano chiles, stems removed, thinly sliced	1–4	2–8	3–10
tomatoes, puréed	2 medium	4 medium	5 medium
unsalted tomato paste	2 Tbsp	3 Tbsp	¼ cup
green or yellow raisins, soaked in just enough water to cover them until ready to use	¼ cup	½ cup	1 cup
garam masala	2 tsp	1 Tbsp + 1 tsp	2 Tbsp
ground coriander	2 tsp	1 Tbsp + 1 tsp	2 Tbsp
amchur (dried mango powder)	2 tsp	1 Tbsp + 1 tsp	2 Tbsp
red chile powder or cayenne pepper	2 tsp	1 Tbsp + 1 tsp	2 Tbsp
kasoori methi (dried fenugreek leaves), lightly hand crushed to release flavor	2 Tbsp	3 Tbsp	¼ cup
salt	1 Tbsp	2 Tbsp	3 Tbsp
russet potatoes, peeled and coarsely chopped	2 medium (3 cups)	4 medium (6 cups)	6 medium (9 cups)
water	5 cups	9 cups	12 cups
chopped fresh cilantro, for garnish	1 Tbsp	2 Tbsp	¼ cup

1. Place the inner pot in your Instant Pot. Select the **SAUTE** setting and adjust to **MORE**. When the indicator flashes **HOT**, add the oil. Once the oil is hot, add the *hing* and cumin. Stir and cook for 1 minute until the seeds turn reddish brown. *Because the oil pools to the sides, push the spices into the oil along the border so they cook fully.*

2. Add the turmeric, cinnamon, cardamom, and cassia or bay leaves. Stir and cook for 30 seconds.

3. Add the onions. Stir and cook for 2 minutes.

4. Add the ginger, garlic, and fresh chiles. Stir and cook for 1 minute.

5. Add the tomatoes and tomato paste. Cook for 1 minute and stir, scraping the bottom of the pot to loosen anything stuck.

6. Press **CANCEL**. Add the raisins along with the soaking water, *garam masala*, coriander, *amchur*, red chile powder, *kasoori methi*, salt, potatoes, and water. Stir. *Including the raisin-soaking water adds a slightly sweet flavor.*

7. Lock the lid into place and make sure the pressure release valve is set to the sealing position (upwards). Press the **PRESSURE COOK** button and then press the **PRESSURE LEVEL** button until the panel reads HIGH. Adjust the cook time to 3 minutes.

8. Once the cooking is complete, release the pressure manually, press **CANCEL**, and remove the lid. Remove and discard the cinnamon, cardamom, and cassia or bay leaves or leave them in for flavor and eat around them. *All the other spices are edible.* Garnish with the cilantro and serve with Indian bread like *puri*, *roti*, or *naan* or with basmati rice. I often add chopped kale, some quinoa, and cooked chickpeas for a filling stew. *You can also use Yukon Gold, red potatoes, or a combination.*

Ginger-Garlic Eggplant

My husband was not an eggplant fan when we first got married. Once he tried this dish, however, he ate it for dinner for almost a week straight. If I can make a convert out of him, I'm sure I can do the same for you and the toughest food critics in your family.

	3 QUART	6 QUART	8 QUART
Yield	4 cups	6 cups	9 cups
Warm up	10 mins	13 mins	16 mins
Cook	3 mins	3 mins	3 mins
Cool down	MR	MR	MR
Total time	13 mins	16 mins	19 mins

Ingredients	3 QUART	6 QUART	8 QUART
oil or *ghee*	1 Tbsp	2 Tbsp	3 Tbsp
hing (asafoetida) (optional)	1 pinch	2 pinches	3 pinches
cumin seeds	1 tsp	2 tsp	1 Tbsp
turmeric powder	1 tsp	2 tsp	1 Tbsp
yellow or red onions, minced	1 small	1 medium	2 medium
piece of ginger, minced	1 (2-inch)	1 (4-inch)	1 (6-inch)
cloves of garlic, minced	10	20	25
fresh Thai or serrano chiles, stems removed, thinly sliced	2–6	4–12	5–14
red chile powder or cayenne pepper	2 tsp	1 Tbsp + 1 tsp	2 Tbsp
salt	2 tsp	1 Tbsp + 1 tsp	3 Tbsp
water	¼ cup	½ cup	¾ cup
eggplant, cut into 1-inch pieces (keep the skin)	6 cups (1 medium)	12 cups (2 medium)	16 cups (3 medium)

1. Place the inner pot in your Instant Pot. Select the **SAUTE** setting and adjust to **NORMAL**. When the indicator flashes **HOT**, add the oil. Once the oil is hot, add the *hing* and cumin. Stir and cook for 40 seconds until the seeds turn reddish brown. *Because the oil pools to the sides, push the spices into the oil along the border so they cook fully.*

2. Add the turmeric. Stir and cook for 30 seconds.

3. Add the onions. Stir and cook for 2 minutes.

4. Add the ginger, garlic, and fresh chiles. Stir and cook for 2 minutes.

5. Add the red chile powder and salt. Stir and cook for 30 seconds.

6. Press **CANCEL**. Carefully remove the inner pot and place it on a heat-resistant surface. Transfer the contents to a bowl, scraping the bottom to loosen anything stuck.

7. Add the water and place a trivet in the pot. Return the pot to the base, add the eggplant, and add the mixture from Step 6 in that order. Do NOT stir.

8. Lock the lid into place. Make sure the pressure release valve is set to the sealing position (upwards). Press the **PRESSURE COOK** button and then press the **PRESSURE LEVEL** button until the panel reads **LOW**. Adjust the cook time to 3 minutes.

9. Once the cooking is complete, release the pressure manually, press **CANCEL**, and remove the lid. Remove the trivet with tongs, stir, and transfer the cooked dish immediately to an unheated container to limit the moisture released. Stir until the eggplant is evenly coated. Serve with basmati rice. *All the spices are edible.*

Fiery Eggplant

From the minute I made this dish, my younger daughter was in love and had two heaping bowls. I'd say that's an endorsement. Baby eggplant can be found in most Indian grocery stores and is just a little sweeter than its larger counterpart. If you can't find it, just substitute regular or Japanese eggplant.

	3 QUART	6 QUART	8 QUART
Yield	4 cups	7 cups	9 cups
Warm up	11 mins	18 mins	16 mins
Cook	6 mins	6 mins	6 mins
Cool down	MR	MR	MR
Total time	17 mins	24 mins	22 mins

Ingredients	3 QUART	6 QUART	8 QUART
baby eggplants, unpeeled and quartered (see note in Step 1)	12	24	30
salt, divided	2 tsp + 1 pinch	4 tsp + 2 pinches	2 Tbsp + 3 pinches
whole tomatoes	1 medium	2 medium	3 medium
piece of ginger, coarsely chopped	1 (2-inch)	1 (4-inch)	1 (6-inch)
cloves of garlic	6	12	15
oil	1 Tbsp	2 Tbsp	3 Tbsp
hing (asafoetida) (optional)	1 pinch	2 pinches	3 pinches
turmeric powder	1 tsp	2 tsp	1 Tbsp
fennel seeds	2 tsp	1 Tbsp + 1 tsp	2 Tbsp
nigella seeds	1 Tbsp	2 Tbsp	3 Tbsp
tomatoes, diced	1 medium	2 medium	3 medium
fresh Thai or serrano chiles, stems removed, thinly sliced	1–6	2–12	3–15
ground coriander	2 Tbsp	4 Tbsp	6 Tbsp
red chile powder or cayenne pepper	2 tsp	1 Tbsp + 1 tsp	2 Tbsp
water	¼ cup	½ cup	¾ cup

1. Place the eggplant in a colander and sprinkle with 1 pinch of salt for a 3-quart IP, 2 pinches of salt for a 6-quart IP, or 3 pinches of salt for an 8-quart IP. Let them stand about 30 minutes to release any bitter juices. Rinse and pat dry. Set aside. *To keep the stems on for presentation, don't cut through the stem end of the eggplant when quartering.*

2. In a food processor, purée the whole tomatoes, ginger, and garlic. Set aside.

3. Place the inner pot in your Instant Pot. Select the **SAUTE** setting and adjust to **MORE**. When the indicator flashes **HOT**, add the oil. Once the oil is hot, add the *hing*, turmeric, fennel, and nigella. Stir and cook for 30 seconds until the seeds turn reddish brown. *Because the oil pools to the sides, push the spices into the oil along the border so they cook fully.*

4. Add the diced tomatoes, fresh chiles, coriander, red chile powder, and the remaining salt. Stir and cook for 1 minute.

5. Add the purée from Step 2. Stir and cook for 2 minutes.

6. Press **CANCEL**. Carefully remove the inner pot and place it on a heat-resistant surface. Transfer the contents to a bowl, scraping the bottom to loosen anything stuck.

7. Return the inner pot to the base, pour in the water, and place a trivet in the pot. Add the eggplant and the mixture from Step 6 in that order. Do NOT stir.

8. Lock the lid into place. Make sure the pressure release valve is set to the sealing position (upwards). Press the **PRESSURE COOK** button and then press the **PRESSURE LEVEL** button until the panel reads **HIGH**. Adjust the cook time to 6 minutes.

9. Once the cooking is complete, release the pressure manually, press **CANCEL**, and remove the lid. Remove the trivet with tongs, stir, and transfer the cooked dish immediately to an unheated container to limit the moisture released. Stir the contents until the eggplant is evenly coated. Serve with Indian bread like *roti* or *naan* or with rice. *All the spices are edible.*

Punjabi Kadhi

Chickpea Flour Curry with Vegetables

Most regions in India have their own version of *kadhi.* The basic ingredients— chickpea flour and yogurt—are the same, but the other ingredients vary depending on where you are from in India. There's a saying that you always prefer *kadhi* the way your mother made it. This Punjabi version is what I grew up eating and loving.

	3 QUART	6 QUART	8 QUART
Yield	8 cups	14 cups	19 cups
Warm up	22 mins	31 mins	28 mins
Cook	15 mins	15 mins	15 mins
Cool down	20 mins NR + MR	20 mins NR + MR	20 mins NR + MR
Total time	57 mins	66 mins	63 mins

Ingredients	3 QUART	6 QUART	8 QUART
plain, unsweetened yogurt (dairy or alternative)	2 cups	4 cups	6 cups
besan (gram or chickpea flour)	1 cup	2 cups	3 cups
turmeric powder	1 Tbsp	2 Tbsp	3 Tbsp
oil or *ghee*	1 Tbsp	2 Tbsp	3 Tbsp
hing (asafoetida) (optional)	1 pinch	2 pinches	3 pinches
cumin seeds	1 tsp	2 tsp	1 Tbsp
whole dried red chiles, broken in pieces	4	8	10
fenugreek seeds	1 tsp	2 tsp	1 Tbsp
yellow or red onions, puréed	1 small	1 medium	2 medium
diced vegetables (eggplant, potato, cauliflower) (optional)	½ cup	1 cup	1½ cups
piece of ginger, puréed	1 (1-inch)	1 (2-inch)	1 (3-inch)
cloves of garlic, puréed	3	6	8
fresh Thai or serrano chiles, stems removed, thinly sliced	1–4	2–8	3–9
water	5 cups	10 cups	13 cups
red chile powder or cayenne pepper	1 Tbsp	2 Tbsp	3 Tbsp
salt	1 Tbsp	2 Tbsp	3 Tbsp

1. Put the yogurt, *besan*, and turmeric in that order in a blender. Process until smooth on low to avoid frothing. *You can also whisk the ingredients in a bowl, but a blender helps break down the flour and gives the dish a smoother finish. Avoid Greek yogurt, which is too thick.*

2. Place the inner pot in your Instant Pot. Select the **SAUTE** setting and adjust to **MORE**. When the indicator flashes **HOT**, add the oil. Once the oil is hot, add the *hing* and cumin. Stir and cook for 40 seconds until the seeds turn reddish brown. *Because the oil pools to the sides, push the spices into the oil along the border so they cook fully.*

3. Add the dried chiles and fenugreek. Stir and cook for 20 seconds. *Do not overcook or the fenugreek will get bitter.*

4. Add the onions and vegetables if using. Stir and cook for 1 minute.

5. Add the ginger, garlic, and fresh chiles. Stir and cook for 1 minute.

6. Press **CANCEL**. Add the water and stir, scraping the bottom to loosen anything stuck. *This will help prevent a burn warning later.*

7. Carefully pour in the yogurt mixture from Step 1. Add the red chile powder and salt. Stir.

8. Lock the lid into place and make sure the pressure release valve is set to the sealing position (upwards). Press the **PRESSURE COOK** button and then press the **PRESSURE LEVEL** button until the panel reads **HIGH**. Adjust the cook time to 15 minutes.

9. Once the cooking is complete, release the pressure naturally for 20 minutes. Then manually release the remaining pressure, press **CANCEL**, and remove the lid. Stir and serve with basmati rice. Kadhi *is traditionally served with* pakoras *(fried chickpea flour dumplings), which are added at the end. When I am short on time, I make this dish without vegetables or* pakoras, *which is just as delicious.*

5 MEATS

Meat cooked in an Instant Pot is so tender it literally falls off the bone. In this chapter, I showcase recipes that are also so deep in flavor that your friends and family will beg for more. I know that mine did!

Punjabi Chicken Curry (page 139) >

RECIPES

Punjabi Chicken Curry

When most people think of Indian food, the first dish that comes to mind is a good chicken curry. I went with my husband's childhood version for this recipe. He says the best chicken curry is made with no vegetables. Though many recipes call for chopped cauliflower or carrots, I've tried to remain true to his tastes.

	3 QUART	6 QUART	8 QUART
Yield	4–6 servings	6–8 servings	8–12 servings
Warm up	13 mins	19 mins	28 mins
Cook	10 mins	10 mins	10 mins
Cool down	10 mins NR + MR	10 mins NR + MR	10 mins NR + MR
Total time	marinate + 33 mins	marinate + 39 mins	marinate + 48 mins

Ingredients	3 QUART	6 QUART	8 QUART
plain, unsweetened yogurt (dairy or alternative)	½ cup	1 cup	1½ cups
garam masala	1 Tbsp	2 Tbsp	3 Tbsp
red chile powder or cayenne pepper	1 Tbsp	2 Tbsp	3 Tbsp
ground coriander	1 Tbsp	2 Tbsp	3 Tbsp
kasoori methi (dried fenugreek leaves), lightly hand crushed to release flavor (optional)	2 Tbsp	¼ cup	¾ cup
salt	1 Tbsp	1 Tbsp + 2 tsp	2 Tbsp
bone-in skinless chicken (drumsticks, thighs, breast; boneless can also be used)	2 lb	4 lb	6 lb
oil or ghee	2 Tbsp	¼ cup	¾ cup
hing (asafoetida) (optional)	1 pinch	2 pinches	3 pinches
cumin seeds	2 tsp	1 Tbsp	1 Tbsp + 1 tsp
turmeric powder	½ tsp	1 tsp	2 tsp
whole cloves	3	6	8
cinnamon stick	1 (2-inch)	1 (2-inch)	1 (3-inch)
cassia leaves (or bay leaves)	½ (or 2)	2 (or 3)	2 (or 3)
yellow or red onions, puréed	1 small	1 medium	2 medium
piece of ginger, puréed	1 (1-inch)	1 (2-inch)	1 (3-inch)
cloves of garlic, puréed	3	6	8
fresh Thai or serrano chiles, stems removed, thinly sliced	2–4	4–8	6–16
tomatoes, puréed	1 medium	2 medium	3 medium
unsalted tomato paste	1 Tbsp	2 Tbsp	3 Tbsp
water	1 cup	2 cups	2½ cups

1. In a large mixing bowl add the yogurt, *garam masala*, red chile powder, coriander, *kasoori methi*, and salt. Stir. Add the chicken and stir until all the pieces are coated. Cover and place in the refrigerator to marinate for 1 hour to overnight. *When you are ready to cook, set the bowl of marinated chicken on the counter to slowly return to room temperature.*

2. Place the inner pot in your Instant Pot. Select the **SAUTE** setting and adjust to **MORE**. When the indicator flashes **HOT**, add the oil. Once the oil is hot, add the *hing* and cumin. Stir and cook for 40 seconds until the seeds turn reddish brown. *Because the oil pools to the sides, push the spices into the oil along the border so they cook fully.*

3. Add the turmeric, cloves, cinnamon, and cassia or bay leaves. Stir and cook for 30 seconds.

4. Add the onions. Stir and cook for 3 minutes in a 3- or 6-quart IP or 4 minutes in an 8-quart IP.

5. Add the ginger, garlic, and fresh chiles. Stir and cook for 1 minute in a 3-quart IP or 2 minutes in a 6- or 8-quart IP.

6. Add the tomatoes and tomato paste. Stir and cook for 1 minute in a 3-quart IP or 2 minutes in a 6- or 8-quart IP.

7. Press **CANCEL**. Add the water and stir, scraping the bottom to loosen anything stuck. *If you prefer less sauce, reduce the water by ¼ cup.*

8. Add the chicken along with the excess yogurt marinade and stir. Lock the lid into place and make sure the pressure release valve is set to the sealing position (upwards). Press the **PRESSURE COOK** button and then press the **PRESSURE LEVEL** button until the panel reads **HIGH**. Adjust the cook time to 10 minutes.

9. Once the cooking is complete, release the pressure naturally for 10 minutes. Then manually release the remaining pressure, press **CANCEL**, and remove the lid. Remove the cloves, cinnamon, and cassia or bay leaves or leave them in for flavor and eat around them. *All the other spices are edible.* Serve with basmati rice or Indian bread like *roti* or *naan*.

Chicken *Tikka Masala*

The popularity of this dish in the West, especially in Great Britain, is indisputable. I modified the recipe for the Instant Pot and eliminated the step of grilling the chicken. If you prefer, grill the chicken before adding it. But first try it my way—you may find you like it and don't need to bother with an extra step.

	3 QUART	6 QUART	8 QUART
Yield	4–6 servings	6–8 servings	8–12 servings
Warm up	15 mins	16 mins	17 mins
Cook	15 mins	15 mins	15 mins
Cool down	10 mins NR + MR	10 mins NR + MR	10 mins NR + MR
Total time	marinate + simmer + 40 mins	marinate + simmer + 41 mins	marinate + simmer + 42 mins

Ingredients	3 QUART	6 QUART	8 QUART
plain, unsweetened yogurt (dairy or alternative)	¾ cup	1½ cups	2 cups
lemon juice	1 Tbsp	2 Tbsp	3 Tbsp
piece of ginger, puréed	1 (1-inch)	1 (2-inch)	1 (3-inch)
cloves of garlic, puréed	6	12	15
paprika (unsmoked)	1 Tbsp	2 Tbsp	3 Tbsp
ground cinnamon	2 tsp	1 Tbsp + 1 tsp	2 Tbsp
ground black pepper	2 tsp	1 Tbsp + 1 tsp	2 Tbsp
boneless, skinless chicken, cut into 2-inch pieces, or skinless bone-in pieces	2 lb	4 lb	6 lb
yellow or red onions, coarsely chopped	1 small	1 medium	2 medium
fresh Thai or serrano chiles, stems removed	2–4	4–8	5–9
unsalted tomato paste	¼ cup	½ cup	¾ cup
garam masala	1 Tbsp	2 Tbsp	3 Tbsp
ground coriander	1 Tbsp	2 Tbsp	3 Tbsp
red chile powder or cayenne pepper	1 Tbsp	2 Tbsp	3 Tbsp
salt	1 Tbsp	2 Tbsp	3 Tbsp
light brown sugar	2 tsp	1 Tbsp + 1 tsp	2 Tbsp
blanched sliced almonds (optional)	2 Tbsp	¼ cup	⅓ cup

Ingredients (continued)	3 QUART	6 QUART	8 QUART
water	¾ cup	1½ cups	2 cups
tomatoes, peeled and coarsely chopped	1 medium	2 medium	3 medium
ghee or oil	1 Tbsp	2 Tbsp	3 Tbsp
hing (asafoetida) (optional)	1 pinch	2 pinches	3 pinches
green cardamom pods, crushed slightly with a mortar and pestle (keep the husks)	2	3	4
half-and-half, heavy cream, or plain unsweetened yogurt (dairy or alternative)	¼ cup	½ cup	¾ cup
minced fresh cilantro, for garnish	2 Tbsp	¼ cup	⅓ cup

1. In a large mixing bowl add the yogurt, lemon juice, ginger, garlic, paprika, cinnamon, and black pepper. Stir. Add the chicken and stir until all the pieces are coated. Cover and place in the refrigerator to marinate for 1 hour to overnight. *When you are ready to cook, set the bowl of marinated chicken on the counter to slowly return to room temperature.*

2. In a food processor grind the onions, fresh chiles, tomato paste, *garam masala*, coriander, red chile powder, salt, brown sugar, almonds, and water until smooth. Add the tomatoes and pulse until broken down but not completely smooth. Set aside.

3. Place the inner pot in your Instant Pot. Select the **SAUTE** setting and adjust to **MORE**. When the indicator flashes **HOT**, add the *ghee*, *hing*, and cardamom. Stir and cook until the *ghee* starts to melt, about 40 seconds.

Recipe continues >

Chicken *Tikka Masala*

Continued

~~~~~~

4. Add the mixture from Step 2. Stir and simmer for 5 minutes.

5. Press **CANCEL**. Carefully remove the inner pot and place on a heat-resistant surface. Once it is cool enough to handle, transfer the contents to a bowl. *Be sure to scrape the bottom to loosen anything stuck.*

6. Return the inner pot to the base. Place a trivet in the pot and place the marinated chicken pieces on it. *Discard any marinade left in the bowl.* Pour the *masala* from Step 5 over the chicken. Do NOT stir.

7. Lock the lid into place and make sure the pressure release valve is set to the sealing position (upwards). Press the **PRESSURE COOK** button and then press the **PRESSURE LEVEL** button until the panel reads **LOW**. Adjust the cook time to 15 minutes.

8. Once the cooking is complete, release the pressure naturally for 10 minutes. Then manually release any remaining pressure, press **CANCEL**, and remove the lid. Let the pot sit uncovered for 2–3 minutes to slightly cool. Remove the trivet with tongs, add the cream, and stir until all the chicken pieces are coated. *The cream holds up better if your dish cools slightly.* Garnish with the cilantro and serve with basmati rice or Indian bread like *roti* or *naan*. For added flavor and crunch, garnish with sliced fresh onion and fresh chiles. *All the spices, including the cardamom husks, are edible, but remove and discard the husks if you prefer.*

Murg Makhani

Butter Chicken

It took me more than two dozen tries to perfect this dish in the Instant Pot and get to the point where my family prefers it over the restaurant version. Making it at home means that you don't have to overload it with butter or cream, so you can feel less guilty about eating it and feeding it to your family.

	3 QUART	6 QUART	8 QUART
Yield	4–6 servings	6–8 servings	8–12 servings
Warm up	8 mins	14 mins	16 mins
Cook	15 mins	15 mins	15 mins
Cool down	10 mins NR + MR	10 mins NR + MR	10 mins NR + MR
Total time	33 mins	39 mins	41 mins

Ingredients	3 QUART	6 QUART	8 QUART
ghee or unsalted butter (dairy or alternative)	4 Tbsp	6 Tbsp	8 Tbsp
green cardamom pods, lightly crushed (keep the husks)	1	2	3
black cardamom pods (no need to crush)	1	2	3
cloves, finely ground	6	12	15
cassia leaves (or bay leaves)	1 (or 2)	2 (or 3)	2 (or 4)
almond flour	¼ cup	½ cup	⅔ cup
turmeric powder	½ tsp	1 tsp	2 tsp
yellow or red onions, puréed	1 small	1 medium	2 medium
piece of ginger, puréed	1 (2-inch)	1 (4-inch)	1 (6-inch)
cloves of garlic, puréed	6	12	15
fresh Thai or serrano chiles, stems removed, thinly sliced	2–4	4–8	8–16
garam masala	2 tsp	1 Tbsp + 1 tsp	2 Tbsp
ground cumin	2 tsp	1 Tbsp + 1 tsp	2 Tbsp
red chile powder or cayenne pepper	2 tsp	1 Tbsp + 1 tsp	2 Tbsp
paprika (unsmoked)	2 tsp	1 Tbsp + 1 tsp	2 Tbsp
light brown sugar	2 tsp	1 Tbsp + 1 tsp	2 Tbsp
salt	1 Tbsp	2 Tbsp	3 Tbsp
water	¼ cup	½ cup	¾ cup

Ingredients (continued)	3 QUART	6 QUART	8 QUART
boneless, skinless chicken breasts, cut into 2-inch pieces	2 lb	4 lb	8 lb
tomatoes, puréed	1 medium	2 medium	3 medium
unsalted tomato paste	1 Tbsp	2 Tbsp	¼ cup
half-and-half or heavy cream (dairy or alternative)	¼ cup	½ cup	⅔ cup
chopped fresh cilantro, for garnish	2 Tbsp	¼ cup	⅓ cup

1. Place the inner pot in your Instant Pot. Select the **SAUTE** setting and adjust to **NORMAL**. When the indicator flashes **HOT**, add the *ghee*, green and black cardamom, cloves, and cassia or bay leaves. Stir and cook for 1 minute.

2. Add the flour. Stir and cook for 40 seconds. *You can also add ½ cup of ground blanched almonds or use all-purpose or quinoa flour instead.*

3. Add the turmeric. Stir and cook for 30 seconds.

4. Add the onions. Stir and cook for 1 minute.

5. Add the ginger, garlic, and fresh chiles. Stir and cook for 1 minute.

6. Add the *garam masala*, cumin, red chile powder, paprika, brown sugar, and salt. Stir and cook for 1 minute.

7. Press **CANCEL**. Carefully remove the inner pot and place on a heat-resistant surface. Once cool enough to handle, transfer the contents to a bowl. *Scrape the bottom to loosen anything stuck—use a tablespoon of water and warm the pot on the SAUTE setting to help deglaze if needed.*

Recipe continues >

Murg Makhani

Continued

8. Return the inner pot to the base. Add the water and then place a trivet in the pot. Place the chicken on the trivet and then add the mixture from Step 7 on top of the chicken. Do NOT stir.

9. Add the tomatoes and tomato paste. *Again, do not stir—the key is to prevent the tomatoes from touching the bottom during the cooking process.*

10. Lock the lid into place and make sure the pressure release valve is set to the sealing position (upwards). Press the **PRESSURE COOK** button and then press the **PRESSURE LEVEL** button until the panel reads **LOW**. Adjust the cook time to 15 minutes.

11. Once the cooking is complete, release the pressure naturally for 10 minutes. Then manually release any remaining pressure, press **CANCEL**, and remove the lid. Let the dish cool for 2–3 minutes and then remove the trivet with tongs and stir until all the chicken is coated. Remove and discard the green cardamom husks, the black cardamom, and cassia or bay leaves or leave them in for flavor and eat around them. *All the other spices are edible.* Add the cream and stir. *The cream holds up better once the dish cools slightly.* Garnish with the cilantro and serve with basmati rice or Indian bread like *roti* or *naan*.

Chicken *Vindaloo*

This dish originated in Goa, and its use of vinegar—and originally, pork, wine, and garlic—is a clear indication of its Portuguese roots. Perfecting this dish in the Instant Pot took a few extra steps that are more than worth it and are critical to get the flavors to come together in a perfectly deep and memorable way.

	3 QUART	6 QUART	8 QUART
Yield	4–6 servings	6–8 servings	8–12 servings
Warm up	14 mins	15 mins	14 mins
Cook	15 mins	15 mins	15 mins
Cool down	5 mins NR + MR	5 mins NR + MR	5 mins NR + MR
Total time	roast + marinate + 34 mins	roast + marinate + 35 mins	roast + marinate + 34 mins

Ingredients	3 QUART	6 QUART	8 QUART
cumin seeds	1 tsp	2 tsp	1 Tbsp
black mustard seeds	2 tsp	1 Tbsp + 1 tsp	1 Tbsp + 2 tsp
whole black peppercorns	2 tsp	1 Tbsp + 1 tsp	2 Tbsp
whole dried red chiles, broken into pieces	4	8	10
vegetable oil, divided	3 Tbsp	4 Tbsp	6 Tbsp
thinly sliced yellow or red onions, divided	4 cups	8 cups	10 cups
piece of ginger, puréed	1 (2-inch)	1 (4-inch)	1 (5-inch)
cloves of garlic, puréed	8	16	20
fresh Thai or serrano chiles, stems removed, thinly sliced	1–3	2–6	3–7
distilled white or apple cider vinegar	3 Tbsp	6 Tbsp	8 Tbsp
light brown sugar	2 tsp	1 Tbsp + 1 tsp	2 Tbsp
ground coriander	2 tsp	1 Tbsp + 1 tsp	2 Tbsp
ground cinnamon	2 tsp	1 Tbsp + 1 tsp	2 Tbsp
red chile powder or cayenne pepper	2 tsp	1 Tbsp + 1 tsp	2 Tbsp
paprika (unsmoked)	1 Tbsp	1 Tbsp + 1 tsp	2 Tbsp
salt	1 Tbsp	2 Tbsp	3 Tbsp
boneless, skinless chicken, cut into 2-inch pieces	2 lb	4 lb	6 lb
turmeric powder	1 tsp	2 tsp	1 Tbsp
tomatoes, diced	1 medium	2 medium	3 medium
tamarind purée	1 Tbsp	2 Tbsp	3 Tbsp
water	¼ cup	½ cup	¾ cup

1. On the stovetop, heat a small, dry pan over medium-high heat. Add the cumin, mustard, peppercorns, and dried chiles. Cook until the spices turn reddish-brown, about 3 minutes. Transfer to a plate and cool for 10 minutes. Grind to a powder with a mortar and pestle or in a spice grinder reserved for spices. Set aside.

2. Place the inner pot in your Instant Pot. Select the **SAUTE** setting and adjust to **MORE**. When the indicator flashes **HOT**, add 2 tablespoons of oil. *In steps 2–5 you prepare the marinade, which can also be made on the stovetop. Use the Instant Pot to avoid cleaning an extra pan.*

3. Once the oil is hot, add 3 cups of onion. Stir and cook until slightly brown, about 15 minutes.

4. Add the ginger, garlic, fresh chiles, and vinegar. Stir and cook for 2 minutes, scraping the bottom to loosen anything stuck.

5. Press **CANCEL** and transfer the onion mixture to a food processor. Process to a smooth paste and transfer to a bowl deep enough to hold the chicken.

6. Add the spice mixture from Step 1, the brown sugar, coriander, cinnamon, red chile powder, paprika, and salt. Stir.

7. Add the chicken, stir until all the pieces are coated, and place it covered in the refrigerator to marinate for 1 hour to overnight. *When you are ready to cook, set the bowl of marinated chicken on the counter to slowly return to room temperature.*

8. Place the inner pot in the Instant Pot. Select the **SAUTE** setting and adjust to **MORE**. When the indicator flashes **HOT**, add the remaining oil. Once the oil is hot, add the turmeric and the remaining onion. Stir and cook for 3 minutes.

9. Add the tomatoes and tamarind. Stir and cook for 2 minutes. Press **CANCEL**. Once cool enough to handle, transfer the contents to a bowl. *Remove anything stuck to the bottom— use a tablespoon of water and warm the pot on the SAUTE setting to help deglaze if needed.*

10. Return the inner pot to the base. Add the water and place a trivet in the pot. Place the chicken with any extra marinade from Step 7 on the trivet. Add the mixture from Step 9 on top of the chicken. Do NOT stir.

11. Lock the lid into place and make sure the pressure release valve is set to the sealing position (upwards). Press the **PRESSURE COOK** button and then press the **PRESSURE LEVEL** button until the panel reads **HIGH**. Adjust the cook time to 15 minutes.

12. Once the cooking is complete, release the pressure naturally for 5 minutes. Then manually release the remaining pressure, press **CANCEL**, and remove the lid. Remove the trivet with tongs, stir, and serve with basmati rice, Indian bread like *roti* or *naan*, or crusty bread. *All the spices are edible.*

Keema

Minced Lamb with Peas

To a Punjabi, *Keema* is pure and simple comfort food. There is something about the minced lamb, the spices, and the oil that pulls together in a magical way. While some recipes for this dish in the Instant Pot call for browning the meat first, I found that it did not make too much of a difference.

	3 QUART	6 QUART	8 QUART
Yield	5 cups	10 cups	14 cups
Warm up	6 mins	18 mins	24 mins
Cook	17 mins	17 mins	17 mins
Cool down	5 mins NR + MR	5 mins NR + MR	5 mins NR + MR
Total time	28 mins	40 mins	46 mins

Ingredients	3 QUART	6 QUART	8 QUART
vegetable oil	2 Tbsp	¼ cup	¼ cup
hing (asafoetida) (optional)	1 pinch	2 pinches	3 pinches
turmeric powder	½ tsp	1 tsp	1½ tsp
cinnamon sticks	1 (2-inch)	2 (2-inch)	3 (2-inch)
cassia leaves (or bay leaves)	1 (or 2)	1 (or 3)	2 (or 4)
yellow or red onions, puréed	1 small	1 medium	2 medium
piece of ginger, puréed	1 (2-inch)	1 (4-inch)	1 (5-inch)
cloves of garlic, puréed	10	20	25
fresh Thai or serrano chiles, stems removed, thinly sliced	2–6	4–12	6–14
ground cumin	2 Tbsp	4 Tbsp	6 Tbsp
ground coriander	2 Tbsp	4 Tbsp	6 Tbsp
garam masala	2 Tbsp	4 Tbsp	6 Tbsp
red chile powder or cayenne pepper	1 Tbsp	2 Tbsp	3 Tbsp
salt	1 Tbsp	2 Tbsp	3 Tbsp
unsalted tomato paste	¼ cup	½ cup	¾ cup
water	¼ cup	½ cup	¾ cup
minced lamb	2 lb	4 lb	6 lb
frozen peas, slightly defrosted	1 cup	2 cups	3 cups
chopped fresh cilantro, for garnish	¼ cup	½ cup	¾ cup

1. Place the inner pot in your Instant Pot. Select the **SAUTE** setting and adjust to **NORMAL**. When the indicator flashes **HOT**, add the oil. Once the oil is hot, add the *hing*, turmeric, cinnamon, and cassia or bay leaves. Stir and cook for 30 seconds. *Because the oil pools to the side, push the spices into the oil along the border so they cook fully.*

2. Add the onions. Stir and cook for 3 minutes.

3. Add the ginger, garlic, and fresh chiles. Stir and cook for 2 minutes.

4. Add the cumin, coriander, *garam masala*, red chile powder, salt, and tomato paste. Stir and cook for 1 minute, scraping the bottom to loosen anything stuck.

5. Press **CANCEL**. Carefully remove the inner pot and place on a heat-resistant surface to cool slightly. Transfer the contents to a bowl. *Be sure to remove anything stuck to the bottom—a tablespoon of water can help.*

6. Return the inner pot to the base, add the water, and place a trivet in the pot. Add the lamb. *It's important to break it down so that it cooks evenly.*

7. Add the mixture from Step 5 and the peas in that order. Press the contents down to make sure they are at or below the maximum fill line. Do NOT stir.

8. Lock the lid into place and make sure the pressure release valve is set to the sealing position (upwards). Press the **PRESSURE COOK** button and then press the **PRESSURE LEVEL** button until the panel reads **HIGH**. Adjust the cook time to 17 minutes.

9. Once the cooking is complete, release the pressure naturally for 5 minutes, manually release the remaining pressure, press **CANCEL**, and remove the lid. Remove the trivet with tongs and stir until the spices are evenly distributed. Remove and discard the cinnamon sticks and cassia or bay leaves or leave them in for flavor and eat around them. *All the other spices are edible.* Garnish with the cilantro and serve with basmati rice or Indian bread like *roti* or *naan*.

Lamb *Biryani*

Biryani is a spiced rice and meat or vegetable dish that may just be the perfect one-pot meal. Spiced and marinated protein or vegetables are cooked with spiced rice and a layering of charred onion, nuts, and dried fruit like raisins. Some of my testers said this version was even better than my stovetop and slow cooker versions.

	3 QUART	6 QUART	8 QUART
Yield	4–6 servings	8–10 servings	10–12 servings
Warm up	24 mins	36 mins	35 mins
Cook	8 mins	8 mins	8 mins
Cool down	NR	NR	NR
Total time	marinate + 32 mins + NR	marinate + 44 mins + NR	marinate + 43 mins + NR

Ingredients	3 QUART	6 QUART	8 QUART
piece of ginger, coarsely chopped	1 (3-inch)	1 (6-inch)	1 (8-inch)
cloves of garlic	4	8	10
fresh Thai or serrano chiles, stems removed	1–3	2–6	3–7
chopped fresh cilantro	¾ cup	1½ cups	2 cups
chopped fresh mint	½ cup	1 cup	1½ cups
plain, unsweetened yogurt (dairy or alternative)	1 cup	2 cups	3 cups
turmeric powder	1 tsp	2 tsp	1 Tbsp
garam masala	2 Tbsp	3 Tbsp	4 Tbsp
red chile powder or cayenne pepper	2 tsp	1 Tbsp + 1 tsp	2 Tbsp
salt, divided	1 Tbsp + 1 pinch	2 Tbsp + 1 pinch	3 Tbsp + 1 pinch
boneless lamb leg or shoulder, cut into 1½-inch cubes	2 lb	4 lb	6 lb
slightly warm milk (dairy or alternative)	2 Tbsp	¼ cup	¾ cup
saffron strands	2 pinches	3 pinches	4 pinches
uncooked basmati rice	2 cups	4 cups	5 cups
ghee or oil	2 Tbsp	3 Tbsp	4 Tbsp
yellow or red onions, thinly sliced	1 medium	2 medium	3 medium
golden or green raisins	1 Tbsp	2 Tbsp	3 Tbsp
nuts (cashews or almonds)	1 Tbsp	2 Tbsp	3 Tbsp
water	1½ cups	3 cups	4 cups

1. In a food processor grind the ginger, garlic, fresh chiles, cilantro, and mint until smooth and place in a bowl large enough to hold the lamb. To the same bowl, add the yogurt, turmeric, *garam masala*, red chile powder, and all but a pinch of the salt. Stir.

2. Add the lamb to this marinade and stir until all the pieces are coated. Refrigerate covered for 1 hour to overnight. *The longer you marinate, the deeper the flavor, but even 1 hour will be delicious. When you are ready to cook, set the bowl of marinated lamb on the counter to slowly return to room temperature.*

3. Pour the milk into a small bowl and sprinkle it with the saffron. Set aside.

4. Rinse the rice and set it aside. *This helps it to soften—there is no need to soak, or it will get mushy.*

5. Place the inner pot in your Instant Pot. Select the **SAUTE** setting and adjust to **MORE**. When the indicator flashes **HOT**, add the *ghee*, onions, and the remaining pinch of salt. Stir and cook until the onions brown, about 15 minutes. Remove with a slotted spoon and set aside.

6. Add the raisins and nuts. Stir and cook for 1–2 minutes until slightly brown. Remove with a slotted spoon and set aside. Press **CANCEL**.

7. Add the marinated lamb plus the marinade, half the onions from Step 5, and the rice in that order. Do NOT stir, just press the rice down with the back of a spatula. Add the other half of the onions and the raisin-nut mixture from Step 6. Pour the water over the rice. Again, do NOT stir.

8. Lock the lid into place and make sure the pressure release valve is set to the sealing position (upwards). Press the **PRESSURE COOK** button and then press the **PRESSURE LEVEL** button until the panel reads **HIGH**. Adjust the cook time to 8 minutes.

9. Once the cooking is complete, release the pressure naturally. *This helps cook the lamb and rice to perfection and pulls the flavors together.* Press **CANCEL** and remove the lid. Add the milk-saffron mixture from Step 3 and then place the lid slightly ajar on the pot for 1–2 minutes so the milk is absorbed. Serve with a side of *raita* (flavored yogurt), mint chutney, and/or topped with a fried egg. *All the spices are edible.*

Lamb *Biryani* (page 149)

Mock *Keema*

Spiced Crumbles with Peas

This dish may be called mock *keema*, but there is nothing to laugh about here.
It is deliciously addictive, and a great way for vegetarians and plant-based eaters to nearly replicate the taste and consistency of traditional *keema*, which is made with lamb. If you've never had vegetarian crumbles, this is a great introduction.

	3 QUART	6 QUART	8 QUART
Yield	5 cups	10 cups	14 cups
Warm up	5 mins	15 mins	22 mins
Cook	8 mins	8 mins	8 mins
Cool down	5 mins NR + MR	5 mins NR + MR	5 mins NR + MR
Total time	18 mins	28 mins	35 mins

Ingredients	3 QUART	6 QUART	8 QUART
vegetable oil	2 Tbsp	¼ cup	¼ cup
hing (asafoetida) (optional)	1 pinch	2 pinches	3 pinches
turmeric powder	½ tsp	1 tsp	1½ tsp
cinnamon sticks	1 (2-inch)	2 (2-inch)	3 (2-inch)
cassia leaves (or bay leaves)	1 (or 2)	1 (or 3)	2 (or 4)
yellow or red onions, puréed	1 small	1 medium	2 medium
piece of ginger, puréed	1 (2-inch)	1 (4-inch)	1 (5-inch)
cloves of garlic, puréed	10	20	25
fresh Thai or serrano chiles, stems removed, thinly sliced	2–6	4–12	6–14
ground cumin	2 Tbsp	4 Tbsp	6 Tbsp
ground coriander	2 Tbsp	4 Tbsp	6 Tbsp
garam masala	2 Tbsp	4 Tbsp	6 Tbsp
red chile powder or cayenne pepper	1 Tbsp	2 Tbsp	3 Tbsp
salt	1 Tbsp	2 Tbsp	3 Tbsp
unsalted tomato paste	¼ cup	½ cup	¾ cup
water	¼ cup	½ cup	¾ cup
meatless grounds (such as those made by Quorn, Boca, or MorningStar Farms)	2 (12-oz) bags	4 (12-oz) bags	6 (12-oz) bags
frozen peas, slightly defrosted	1 cup	2 cups	3 cups
chopped fresh cilantro, for garnish	¼ cup	½ cup	¾ cup

1. Place the inner pot in your Instant Pot. Select the **SAUTE** setting and adjust to **NORMAL**. When the indicator flashes **HOT**, add the oil. Once the oil is hot, add the *hing*, turmeric, cinnamon, and cassia or bay leaves. Stir and cook for 30 seconds. *Because the oil pools to the sides, push the spices into the oil along the border so they cook fully.*

2. Add the onions. Stir and cook for 3 minutes.

3. Add the ginger, garlic, and fresh chiles. Stir and cook for 2 minutes.

4. Add the cumin, coriander, *garam masala*, red chile powder, salt, and tomato paste. Stir and cook for 1 minute, scraping the bottom to loosen anything stuck.

5. Press **CANCEL**. Carefully remove the inner pot and place on a heat-resistant surface to cool slightly. Transfer the contents to a bowl. *Be sure to remove anything stuck to the bottom—a tablespoon of water can help.*

6. Return the inner pot to the base, add the water, and place a trivet in the pot. Add the meatless grounds.

7. Add the mixture from Step 5 and the peas in that order. Press the contents down to make sure they are at or below the maximum fill line. Do NOT stir.

8. Lock the lid into place and make sure the pressure release valve is set to the sealing position (upwards). Press the **PRESSURE COOK** button and then press the **PRESSURE LEVEL** button until the panel reads **HIGH**. Adjust the cook time to 8 minutes.

9. Once the cooking is complete, release the pressure naturally for 5 minutes, manually release the remaining pressure, press **CANCEL**, and remove the lid. Remove the trivet with tongs and stir until the spices are evenly distributed. Remove and discard the cinnamon and cassia or bay leaves or leave them in for flavor and eat around them. *All the other spices are edible.* Garnish with the cilantro and serve with basmati rice or Indian bread like *roti* or *naan*.

Nihari

Beef Stew

While for religious reasons many Hindus do not eat beef, there is a large Muslim community in India that does. This dish is a staple in those communities. It would typically take several hours to cook on the stovetop or in the slow cooker. The Instant Pot cuts that time to a fraction without sacrificing flavor. Keep in mind, the cook time does fluctuate based on the amount of product.

	3 QUART	6 QUART	8 QUART
Yield	6–8 servings	10–12 servings	12–14 servings
Warm up	8 mins	17 mins	19 mins
Cook	60 mins	70 mins	90 mins
Cool down	10 mins NR + MR	10 mins NR + MR	10 mins NR + MR
Total time	browning + 78 mins + simmer	browning + 97 mins + simmer	browning + 119 mins + simmer

Ingredients

Ingredients	3 QUART	6 QUART	8 QUART
ghee or oil, divided	2 Tbsp	4 Tbsp	6 Tbsp
yellow or red onions, thinly sliced	2 medium	3 medium	4 medium
white salt, divided	1¼ tsp	2½ tsp	1 Tbsp
beef brisket or shank, cut into large pieces	2 lb	4 lb	6 lb
piece of ginger, puréed	1 (2-inch)	1 (4-inch)	1 (6-inch)
cloves of garlic, puréed	10	20	30
ground ginger	2 tsp	1 Tbsp + 1 tsp	2 Tbsp
garam masala	1 Tbsp	2 Tbsp	3 Tbsp
ground cardamom seeds	½ tsp	1 tsp	1½ tsp
ground fennel seeds	2 Tbsp	¼ cup	⅓ cup
cinnamon sticks	1 (2-inch)	2 (2-inch)	3 (2-inch)
cassia leaves (or bay leaves)	1 (or 2)	2 (or 3)	2 (or 4)
ground nutmeg	1 tsp	2 tsp	1 Tbsp
turmeric powder	1 tsp	2 tsp	1 Tbsp
kala namak (black salt)	2 tsp	1 Tbsp + 1 tsp	2 Tbsp
red chile powder or cayenne pepper	2 tsp	1 Tbsp + 1 tsp	2 Tbsp
water, divided	2 cups	4 cups	6 cups
chapati or all-purpose flour	¼ cup	½ cup	¾ cup
fresh Thai or serrano chiles, stems removed, thinly sliced	1–6	2–12	3–15
chopped fresh cilantro, for garnish	2 Tbsp	¼ cup	⅓ cup

1. Place the inner pot in your Instant Pot. Select the **SAUTE** setting and adjust to **MORE**. When the indicator flashes **HOT**, add half of the *ghee*, the onions, and ¼ teaspoon of the white salt for a 3-quart IP or ½ teaspoon of the salt for a 6-quart or 8-quart IP. Stir occasionally and cook until the onions brown, about 10 minutes. Press **CANCEL**, move the inner pot to a heat-resistant surface. Using a slotted spoon, transfer the onions to a small bowl. Set aside.

2. Return the inner pot to the base, again select the **SAUTE** setting, and adjust to **MORE**. When the indicator flashes **HOT**, place 1–2 pieces of meat in the pot, sear for 2 minutes on each side, and transfer the pieces to a plate. Repeat until all the pieces have been seared. Set aside. *I prefer to cook the beef in 4-inch by 3-inch chunks so that it stays as juicy as possible. If using a cut of beef with a bone, keep it when cooking for added flavor.*

3. Add the remaining *ghee* to the pot along with the fresh ginger, garlic, ground ginger, *garam masala*, cardamom, fennel, cinnamon, cassia or bay leaves, nutmeg, turmeric, *kala namak*, red chile powder, and the remaining white salt. Stir and cook for 40 seconds. Add half of the water and stir, scraping the bottom to loosen anything stuck.

4. Press **CANCEL**. Add the meat from Step 2 (along with any juice), the remaining water, and the onions from Step 1. Do NOT stir.

5. Lock the lid into place and make sure the pressure release valve is set to the sealing position (upwards). Press the **PRESSURE COOK** button and then press the **PRESSURE LEVEL** button until the panel reads **HIGH**. Adjust the cook time to the time indicated in the chart above.

6. Once the cooking is complete, release the pressure naturally for 10 minutes. Then manually release the remaining pressure, press **CANCEL**, and remove the lid. With tongs, remove the meat and let it sit for 5 minutes before slicing it thin.

7. Remove a portion of the cooked broth (1 cup for a 3-quart IP, 2 cups for a 6-quart IP, or 3 cups for an 8-quart IP) and place it in a bowl. Add the flour and whisk until smooth. Return this mixture to the inner pot. *You can substitute gluten-free flour like quinoa or almond if you prefer.*

8. Select the **SAUTE** setting and adjust to **NORMAL**. Add the fresh chiles, stir, and from the point of simmer, cook uncovered for 5 minutes until the broth thickens. Add the sliced meat and continue to simmer for another 5 minutes.

9. Press **CANCEL**. Remove and discard the cinnamon and cassia or bay leaves or leave them in for flavor and eat around them. *All the other spices are edible.* Garnish with the cilantro and serve with basmati rice, *roti*, or *naan*.

6

SIDES, DESSERTS, & MORE

In this section I give you a variety of recipes that work quite well in the Instant Pot, from an Indian "curry" starter, to yogurt, to dessert like rice pudding and carrot *halwa*. You and your family will love how easy they are to make and how with a little planning, these Indian sides and desserts can be on your table most nights of the week.

Kheer (Rice Pudding) (page 162) >

RECIPES

Gila Masala

Wet Curry Base

Masala refers to mixed spices. *Gila* means wet. Put them together and you have the base for many North Indian dishes. The challenge is getting it to the right consistency—it should never be watery. This can be tough in a pressure cooker where water is necessary. Thus, I employ the pot-in-pot cooking method, which works perfectly.

	3 QUART	6 QUART	8 QUART
Yield	2 cups	4 cups	7 cups
Warm up	5 mins	7 mins	5 mins
Cook	10 mins	10 mins	10 mins
Cool down	NR	NR	NR
Total time	sauté + 15 mins + NR	sauté + 17 mins + NR	sauté + 15 mins + NR

Ingredients	3 QUART	6 QUART	8 QUART
coarsely chopped yellow onions	4 cups (4 medium)	8 cups (8 medium)	12 cups (12 medium)
peeled and coarsely chopped ginger	½ cup (4 inches)	1 cup (8 inches)	1½ cups (12 inches)
cloves of garlic, coarsely chopped	12	24	35
salt	½ tsp	1 tsp	1½ tsp
vegetable oil	½ cup	1 cup	1½ cups
turmeric powder	2 Tbsp	¼ cup	⅓ cup
water, divided	¼ cup + 1 cup	½ cup + 2 cups	½ cup + 2 cups
unsalted tomato paste	¼ cup	½ cup	¾ cup

1. In a food processor, grind the onions until smooth and transfer to a bowl. *As the onion sits, moisture will collect to the sides. Before cooking, drain this moisture and use a slotted spoon to transfer the onion purée to the inner pot. Save the water in the fridge to add to a curry or soup.*

2. In the same food processor (no need to rinse), grind the ginger and garlic together until smooth and transfer to a different bowl.

3. Place the inner pot in your Instant Pot. Select the **SAUTE** setting and adjust to **MORE**. When the indicator flashes **HOT**, add the onion from Step 1 and the salt. *The salt helps pull out extra moisture. Cooking without oil first helps dry up any extra moisture.* Sauté for 5 minutes in a 3-quart IP, 10 minutes in a 6-quart IP, or 20 minutes in an 8-quart IP, stirring occasionally but not too often to allow the onion to brown slightly. *The SAUTE setting is programmed to turn off automatically after 30 minutes. If it does, just restart it.*

4. Add the oil. Stir and sauté for another 5 minutes in a 3-quart IP, 10 minutes in a 6-quart IP, or 15 minutes in an 8-quart IP.

5. Add the ginger-garlic mixture from Step 2 and the turmeric. Stir and sauté for 2 minutes in a 3-quart IP or 4 minutes in a 6-quart or 8-quart IP. *Be sure to stir often so it does not burn.*

6. Press **CANCEL**. Carefully move the inner pot to a heat-resistant surface and transfer the mixture to an oven-safe glass or metal bowl that will fit into the inner pot of the Instant Pot (with the lid). Pour a portion of the water (¼ cup for a 3-quart IP or ½ cup for a 6-quart or 8-quart IP) into the inner pot and scrape the bottom to loosen anything stuck. Pour this into the bowl with the onion mixture. *You can use the metal inner pot of a smaller Instant Pot.*

7. Add the tomato paste to the onion mixture and stir.

8. Return the empty inner pot to the base, pour in the remaining water, put a trivet in the pot, and place the bowl from Step 7 on the trivet.

9. Lock the lid into place. Make sure the pressure release valve is set to the sealing position (upwards). Press the **PRESSURE COOK** button and then press the **PRESSURE LEVEL** button until the panel reads **HIGH**. Adjust the cook time to 10 minutes.

10. Once the cooking is complete, release the pressure naturally, press **CANCEL**, and remove the lid. Very carefully remove the bowl and stir the contents. This mixture will last 2–3 weeks in the fridge and up to 3 months in the freezer. Use about 1 cup of *masala* in any wet dish on the stovetop, from *mattar paneer* (peas and cheese) to meat curries. You can even make other dishes like *chana masala* and *rajmah* in the Instant Pot and use this *masala* for the base curry.

NOTE: If you would like to use fresh tomatoes, substitute 2 medium tomatoes for every ¼ cup of tomato paste. Purée them in the food processor after the ginger and garlic. *No need to peel.* The consistency and color will be slightly different, but it will still be delicious. I prefer making this *masala* without spices so that I can add them later specific to the dish that I am cooking.

Aam Ki Chutney

Mango Chutney

I can't get enough of mango chutney and how easy it is to make in the **Instant Pot.** The key is to cook it through and then sauté it at the end to thicken it slightly. The sweet and savory mix makes this a delicious side for grilled meat, tofu, or veggies or a topping for yogurt or toast.

	3 QUART	6 QUART	8 QUART
Yield	1½ cups	4 cups	5 cups
Warm up	8 mins	13 mins	15 mins
Cook	10 mins	10 mins	10 mins
Cool down	5 mins NR + MR	5 mins NR + MR	5 mins NR + MR
Total time	23 mins + simmer	28 mins + simmer	30 mins + simmer

Ingredients	3 QUART	6 QUART	8 QUART
vegetable oil	1 Tbsp	2 Tbsp	3 Tbsp
whole cloves	6	12	15
cinnamon sticks	1 (2-inch)	2 (2-inch)	3 (2-inch)
shallots, minced	1 small	1 medium	2 medium
piece of ginger, minced	1 (1-inch)	1 (2-inch)	1 (3-inch)
cloves of garlic, minced	2	4	6
red chile powder or cayenne pepper	½ tsp	1 tsp	1½ tsp
salt	2 tsp	1 Tbsp + 1 tsp	1 Tbsp + 2 tsp
ground ginger	½ tsp	1 tsp	1½ tsp
apple cider vinegar or white vinegar	¼ cup	⅓ cup	½ cup
diced mango (fresh or frozen)	4 cups	8 cups	12 cups
light brown sugar	3 Tbsp	6 Tbsp	8 Tbsp

1. Place the inner pot in your Instant Pot. Select the **SAUTE** setting and adjust to **MORE**. When the indicator flashes **HOT**, add the oil, cloves, and cinnamon. Stir and cook for 30 seconds. *Because the oil pools to the sides, push the spices into the oil along the border of the inner pot so they can cook fully.*

2. Add the shallots, fresh ginger, and garlic. Stir and cook for 40 seconds.

3. Press **CANCEL**. Add the red chile powder, salt, ground ginger, and vinegar. Stir, scraping the bottom to loosen anything stuck.

4. Add the mango and stir. Add the sugar. Do NOT stir.

5. Lock the lid into place. Make sure the pressure release valve is set to the sealing position (upwards). Press the **PRESSURE COOK** button and then press the **PRESSURE LEVEL** button until the panel reads **HIGH**. Adjust the cook time to 10 minutes.

6. Once the cooking is complete, release the pressure naturally for 5 minutes. Then manually release the remaining pressure, press **CANCEL**, and remove the lid.

7. Select the **SAUTE** setting and adjust to **MORE**. Simmer uncovered for 8–10 minutes until the chutney thickens slightly. Stir frequently so that it does not burn. When finished, press **CANCEL** and transfer the inner pot to a heat-resistant surface to cool for 10 minutes. Remove and discard the cloves and cinnamon or leave in for flavor and eat around them. Transfer the chutney to a container and refrigerate, or alternatively, store in ice-cube trays in the freezer. *If the chutney burns slightly, avoid scraping the bottom when transferring.*

NOTE: If using frozen mango, let it sit and slightly defrost as you prep. Substitute any sweetener you like for the brown sugar, including *gur* (jaggery).

TRY THIS! Add any dried fruit including raisins, cherries, or cranberries along with the mango. Serve alongside grilled meats like chicken or lamb.

Dahi

Homemade Yogurt

	3 QUART	6 QUART	8 QUART
Yield	7 cups	14 cups	20 cups
Warm up	30 mins	30 mins	30 mins
Cool down	30+ mins	40+ mins	40+ mins
Incubate	8 hours	8 hours	8 hours
Total time	9 hours + refrigeration	9 hours 10 mins + refrigeration	9 hours 10 mins + refrigeration

Indians love their yogurt—light, tangy, and mixed with spices and grated veggies like cucumbers, carrots, and onions. I have tried my family's techniques for years to make yogurt the way they do, but for some reason, it would not set consistently for me. Until now. The Instant Pot changed all the uncertainty with one simple push of a button.

Ingredients	3 QUART	6 QUART	8 QUART
milk (whole, low-fat, or skim)	8 cups (½ gallon)	16 cups (1 gallon)	22 cups (1 gallon + 6 cups)
natural, live/active-culture plain yogurt	2 Tbsp	¼ cup	½ cup

NOTE: Although making yogurt is simple, getting the right starter can be a challenge. You can use store-bought yogurt as your starter, but keep in mind that your final product will taste like the starter. Indian yogurt is slightly thinner and tart. If you have an Indian friend, ask them for a bit of their yogurt. Or look for cartons labeled "Desi" yogurt in the refrigerated section of Indian grocery stores.

NOTE: To make *hung* curd, a thicker consistency used in dips, marinades, desserts, and sometimes *raita*, simply drain the yogurt for 1–2 hours. For thicker, Greek-style yogurt, drain it overnight. You can use cheesecloth positioned in a colander over a bowl, but the easier way is to use almond milk draining bags which can be washed and reused. Place the yogurt in a bag and set it in a container slightly elevated to drain in the fridge. I place a trivet in the inner pot of an Instant Pot, place the bag of yogurt on the trivet, and place the pot in the fridge. Be sure to drain after a few hours so the yogurt bag never sits in the drained liquid (whey). This liquid can be discarded or saved in the fridge or frozen in ice-cube trays to be added to curries or smoothies.

1. Place the inner pot in your Instant Pot. Select the **SAUTE** setting and adjust to **NORMAL**.

2. Pour the milk into the pot and wait for it to come to a slow boil. This will take about 30 minutes. *It's important that the milk is hot, but that you don't boil it too long—it can stick to the bottom of the pot. Be careful it does not boil over.*

3. As soon as the milk comes to a boil, press **CANCEL** and carefully transfer the pot to a heat-resistant surface to cool for 30–40 minutes until the milk is lukewarm. *If a slight layer of cream (*malai*) forms on top, just scrape it off and save it to eat later or discard it. The milk should be about 110 degrees Fahrenheit. I just touch it with one finger and if it's warm to the touch it's fine.*

4. Transfer 1 cup of this milk to a bowl. Add the yogurt culture and whisk until blended. Pour this mixture back into the pot with the warm milk and stir. *Be careful not to scrape the bottom in case some milk is stuck.*

5. Either place a glass lid on the pot or use the Instant Pot lid. Make sure the release valve is in the venting position (downward). Press the **YOGURT** button. It will automatically incubate for 8 hours.

6. When finished, remove the lid. Transfer the inner pot to the refrigerator, cover, and allow it to set for 6 hours to overnight. Store as is or transfer to glass or metal containers for up to 2 weeks in the fridge. Enjoy as a *raita* with chopped or grated veggies, salt, pepper, and spices or blended with fruit and a touch of honey. This also makes a wonderful base for *lassi*, an Indian yogurt-based drink.

TRY THIS! Pour the milk-culture mixture into heat-safe glass or metal containers and position them in the pressure cooker before incubating. When you are finished, place a lid on the jars and refrigerate. I prefer to make a larger quantity in the inner pot and then dole it into glass jars.

Kheer

Rice Pudding

There is something universal and comforting about rice pudding, and *kheer* is no exception. Where my Instant Pot recipe differs from others is that I pull back on the amount of milk used. This, to my dad, who is a *kheer* aficionado, made all the difference.

	3 QUART	6 QUART	8 QUART
Yield	3½ cups	8 cups	12 cups
Warm up	13 mins	19 mins	21 mins
Cook	20 mins	20 mins	20 mins
Cool down	NR	NR	NR
Total time	33 mins + NR	39 mins + NR	41 mins + NR

Ingredients	3 QUART	6 QUART	8 QUART
ghee or vegetable oil, divided	1 Tbsp	2 Tbsp	3 Tbsp
ground green cardamom seeds or powder	½ tsp	1 tsp	1½ tsp
golden or green raisins or diced dried fruit, soaked in water	2 Tbsp	¼ cup	⅓ cup
uncooked white basmati rice, washed (not soaked)	½ cup	1 cup	1½ cups
sugar	⅓ cup	⅔ cup	1 cup
milk (whole, low-fat, skim, or dairy alternative)	3½ cups	7 cups	11 cups
finely chopped slivered almonds or pistachios, for garnish	2 Tbsp	¼ cup	⅓ cup

1. Coat the inner pot with one-third of the *ghee* or oil or use a spray oil. *This helps prevent the milk from boiling up the sides during cooking.*

2. Place the inner pot in your Instant Pot. Select the **SAUTE** setting and adjust to **MORE**.

3. When the indicator flashes **HOT**, add the remaining *ghee*. When the *ghee* melts/is hot, add the cardamom and drained raisins. Stir and cook for 30 seconds.

4. Add the rice and sugar. Stir and cook for 30 seconds.

5. Press **CANCEL**. Carefully add the milk and stir.

6. Lock the lid into place. Make sure the pressure release valve is set to the sealing position (upwards). Press the **PRESSURE COOK** button and then press the **PRESSURE LEVEL** button until the panel reads **HIGH**. Adjust the cook time to 20 minutes. *If you prefer your rice to be cooked a little less, reduce the cook time by 3 to 4 minutes. If you are using jasmine rice, cook 15 minutes.*

7. Once the cooking is complete, release the pressure naturally, press **CANCEL**, and remove the lid. *If you release the steam manually, the milk will splatter. A natural release also helps to thicken your dish and create the perfect consistency.* Leave the *kheer* uncovered in the pot to cool for another 10 minutes. *This is another step that helps create a slightly thicker consistency.* Either serve warm or chill in the fridge first. Dole into bowls and garnish with chopped nuts.

NOTE: *Ghee* gives the finished product a warmer hue and a slightly richer taste. With oil, your kheer will be brighter and whiter. The rice you use can make a big difference. I tested this recipe with long-grain basmati. If you use a shorter-grain rice, you may need to reduce the cook time to 15 minutes and sometimes less. Heavier, non-dairy milk can be substituted including soy and oat. Because almond milk has a higher water content, reduce the cook time to 15 minutes if using.

TRY THIS! If you want to elevate the hue and taste of your *kheer*, add a pinch or two of saffron along with the cardamom and raisins in Step 3.

Gajar ka Halwa or Gajrela

Carrot *Halwa*

	3 QUART	6 QUART	8 QUART
Yield	2 cups	4 cups	5 cups
Warm up	6 mins	8 mins	8 mins
Cook	8 mins + 27 mins sauté	8 mins + 27 mins sauté	8 mins + 37 mins sauté
Cool down	4 mins NR + MR	4 mins NR + MR	4 mins NR + MR
Total time	45 mins	47 mins	57 mins

I remember my mother spending all day cooking this dessert on the stove. The pot would rattle, sometimes the milk would boil over, and she'd constantly have to adjust the heat. The Instant Pot is truly a game changer. What I like most is that you can combine the art of sauteing and pressure cooking all in one pot with virtually no mess.

Ingredients	3 QUART	6 QUART	8 QUART
ghee or vegetable oil, divided	2 Tbsp	4 Tbsp	6 Tbsp
raw, unsalted cashews	2 Tbsp	¼ cup	½ cup
hand-grated carrots	4 cups (4 large)	8 cups (8 large)	12 cups (12 large)
milk (whole, low-fat, skim, or dairy alternative)	½ cup	1 cup	1½ cups
sugar	⅔ cup	1⅓ cups	1¾ cups
dried milk (whole, low-fat, skim, or dairy alternative)	¼ cup	½ cup	½ cup
ground green cardamom seeds or powder	½ tsp	1 tsp	1½ tsp

1. Place the inner cooking pot in your Instant Pot. Select the **SAUTE** setting and adjust to **MORE**. When the indicator flashes **HOT**, add half of the *ghee*.

2. When the *ghee* has melted, add the cashews. Stir and cook for 30 seconds. Carefully remove the inner pot so it doesn't get too hot and transfer the cashews to a small bowl with a slotted spoon, leaving the *ghee* behind. Set the cashews aside.

3. Return the inner pot to the base, add the carrots, and **SAUTE** for 6 minutes. Stir often so that the carrots do not stick. *While it's more work, hand-grated carrots are essential. A food processor or pre-grated carrots will not be thin enough and the consistency will be off.*

4. Press **CANCEL**. Add the milk and stir. Lock the lid into place. Make sure the pressure release valve is set to the sealing position (upwards). Press the **PRESSURE COOK** button and then press the **PRESSURE LEVEL** button until the panel reads **HIGH**. Adjust the cook time to 8 minutes.

5. Once the cooking is complete, release the pressure naturally for 4 minutes and then release the remaining pressure manually. Press **CANCEL** and open the lid.

6. Press the **SAUTE** button and adjust to **MORE**. Add the sugar and stir. From the point of simmer, cook uncovered for 15 minutes in a 3- or 6-quart IP or 25 minutes in an 8-quart IP, stirring often to make sure the carrots don't stick or burn. *If the pot gets too hot, turn the setting to NORMAL. This uncovered cook time is critical to evaporate the extra moisture.*

7. Add the dried milk. Cook for 3 minutes and stir regularly to make sure nothing sticks to the bottom or burns. *The* halwa *will start to pull away from the sides of the pot. If it starts to stick to the bottom, add 1–2 teaspoons of milk and stir.*

8. Add the remaining *ghee* and cook for another 3 minutes, stirring often.

9. Press **CANCEL**. Carefully move the inner pot to a heat-resistant surface, add the cashews from Step 2 and the cardamom, and stir. Cool for 5 minutes. Either serve warm (alone or with vanilla ice cream) or chill in the fridge first.

Essential Sides

Rice: The key to making fluffy rice is to get the proportion between the rice and water right. For white rice, including basmati, use double the amount of water. So, for 1 cup rice, use 2 cups water. For brown rice, use double plus 1 extra cup of water. So, for 1 cup brown rice, use 3 cups water.

To add an Indian touch to the rice, heat 1 tablespoon oil over medium-high heat and add about half of 1 medium onion sliced, 2 whole cloves, 2 large black cardamom pods, and 1 stick of cinnamon. Brown the onions slightly and add 1 cup of rice, 2 teaspoons of sea salt, and 2 cups of water. Cover the pan with a lid, making sure to leave it slightly ajar to let the steam out. Cook for about 20 minutes, until the water evaporates.

Roti/Naan: *Naan* can be found in most grocery stores, while *roti*, also called *chapati* or *phulka*, is more readily available at an Indian grocer. Keep in mind that *roti* is the healthiest option, as it's made with whole-wheat flour. *Naan* can also be healthy if you purchase a whole-wheat version.

To make my own *roti*, I usually mix the dough in my food processor. The proportion that works best for me is 3 cups *aata* to 1½ cups water and 1 tablespoon vegetable oil. I blend the mixture until it becomes a sticky ball, much like pizza dough. Then I knead it on my clean countertop, which has been prepped with a thin layer of dry *aata*. Pull off small balls, about 2 inches in diameter, dip them into dry *aata*, and roll them out with a rolling pin into thin circles. Cook on a preheated, flat frying pan until browned on both sides. Stack the *rotis* as you finish cooking them. They'll keep in the fridge for about 1 week. Use 100 percent whole-wheat *chapati* flour from an Indian grocery store for the best results.

Yogurt/Raita: Indians generally eat plain, savory yogurt. To add some basic Indian touches, add a pinch each of sea salt, black salt, and red chile powder to a cup of plain, unsweetened yogurt and serve it with your Indian meal.

To make a *raita*, follow the same instructions, but also add anything from grated cucumber, to chopped onions and tomatoes, to pomegranate seeds. Anything is possible, and the more you experiment, the more variations you'll come up with.

Chutneys: Mint chutney is probably the most common Indian chutney. To make it, take a large bunch of mint leaves, remove and discard the hard stems, and grind them in a blender or food processor with a small piece of peeled ginger, 2 cloves garlic, 1 small chopped onion, 2 small fresh chiles, sea salt, red chile powder, and a little lemon juice. To jazz it up a bit, substitute fresh cilantro for half the mint leaves.

Indian Onion Salads are my passion. I have to have raw, fresh onions with my meal or I don't feel like I've actually eaten. For a basic salad, put sliced raw onions, sliced cucumbers, and sliced tomatoes on a large plate. Sprinkle with sea salt, black salt, and red chile powder. Squeeze half a lemon over the top and serve.

Burnt Onions: Finely chop 1 large yellow or red onion. Heat 3 tablespoons vegetable oil in a frying pan over medium-high heat. Stirring occasionally, cook until the onion is dark brown. Sprinkle over dishes before serving. This topping can last in the fridge for up to 2 weeks. It will soften a bit but will still be delicious as a topping to any dish.

INDEX